THE MODERN QUILTING BEE

block party

The Journey of 12 Women, 1 Blog & 12 Improvisational Projects

Alissa Haight Carlton
& Kristen Lejnieks

stash BOOKS®

an imprint of C&T Publishing

Publisher: Amy Marson

Creative Director: Gailen Runge

Acquisitions Editor: Susanne Woods

Editor: Cynthia Bix

Technical Editor: Susan Nelsen

Copyeditor/Proofreader: Wordfirm Inc.

Cover/Book Designer: Kristy Zacharias

Production Coordinator: Jenny Leicester

Production Editor: Julia Cianci

Illustrator: Mary E. Flynn

Photography by Christina Carty-Francis and Diane Pedersen of C&T Publishing, Inc., unless otherwise noted

Published by Stash Books, an imprint of C&T Publishing, Inc., P.O. Box 1456, Lafayette, CA 94549

Library of Congress Cataloging-in-Publication Data

Carlton, Alissa Haight, 1976-

 Block party--the modern quilting bee : the journey of 12 women, 1 blog & 12 improvisational projects / Alissa Haight Carlton and Kristen Lejnieks.

  p. cm.

 ISBN 978-1-60705-197-8 (softcover)

 1. Quilting--Patterns. 2. Quilting--Blogs. I. Lejnieks, Kristen, 1980- II. Title.

 TT835.C374135 2011

 746.46--dc22

                    2010039158

Printed in China

10 9 8 7 6 5 4 3 2 1

ACKNOWLEDGMENTS

FROM ALISSA:

I would like to thank my wonderful husband, Gavin, for being so supportive throughout the process of working on this book. I can't begin to count the days when sewing and writing were the priority, and I will forever be thankful for his patience. I'm eternally grateful to have such a giving and loving partner in life.

I'd also like to thank my family, who are all so encouraging—especially my twin sister, Cate, who is my best friend and biggest fan; my sister Sarah, who is constantly interested and enthusiastic; and my brother, Steve, for putting up with all his sisters.

Of course a huge thank-you also goes to my parents: my mother, from whom I got the skills to sew and who is always there to listen or give advice when it's needed, and my father, from whom I got the skills to write and who always lets me know that he's proud of me.

Lastly, I have to thank my friends, both in "real" life and in the quilting community—especially Kasha, for being my endless cheerleader. All of your friendships and quilting inspirations are invaluable!

FROM KRISTEN:

I would like to dedicate this book to my two girls, Annabelle and Matilda. I was inspired to start sewing again during my first pregnancy, and my children continue to be my biggest source of inspiration. I hope Annie and Tilda can find their passion in life as I have found mine.

I would also like to thank my husband, Joe. He has served as a constant source of support, and I do not think this book could have been written without him. It was always a challenge to try to write and sew while also having a full-time job, and it is Joe who made this possible.

Finally, I owe a huge debt of gratitude to my entire extended family—Mom, Dad, Steve, Jayne, Dani, Christina, Theresa, Emily, and Steven. I am particularly grateful to my mom, who first taught me to sew. She has sewn her entire life—quilts, costumes, curtains, and clothing—and I thank her for passing that gift on to me.

FROM KRISTEN AND ALISSA:

Many thanks to Robert Kaufman Fabrics and to Art Gallery Fabrics for supplying us with wonderful fabrics. Thanks also to The Warm Company for fabulous batting.

We'd both like to thank the whole team at C&T for their work and support on this book: Susanne, Cynthia, Susan, Kristy, Jenny, Julia, Mary, and all others who were involved.

Your guidance has been immeasurably helpful. Thank you.

january

february

march

april

may

june

july

august

september

october

november

december

contents

foreword

by Denyse Schmidt

Many Hands Make Light Work

One of the things that made me fall in love with quilting was the idea of the quilting bee. I had recently moved to a new state after art school to live with a new boyfriend, who—in the sudden context of complete newness and unfamiliarity with every aspect of my life—I realized I barely knew. I had no close friends in the immediate area, and as this was long before the Internet and email, I felt rather lonely and isolated initially. At the time, I was hand-quilting a traditional Nine Patch for said boyfriend, and learning about the history of the craft. The notion of women in rural farming or pioneer communities getting together to make light work of what was an enormously time-consuming undertaking, while sharing their stories and friendship along with music, dancing, and food, sounded like heaven to me.

I thought about the lives of these women—early marriage to relative strangers, months of isolation, relentless chores, and very few opportunities to swap tales and enjoy the perspective that comes from sharing experiences. My life was certainly not so extreme, but the nostalgic concept of the quilting bee struck a chord I was longing for, and it stuck. (In fact, it stuck around a lot longer than that boyfriend!) Over the years, relationships have come and gone and I've relocated several times, but my love of quilting remains constant. What began as a hobby became my life's work.

So welcome to the quilting community and this wonderful tradition of collaboration and friendship—where the whole truly is greater than the sum of its parts.

A virtual quilting bee or block swap offers inspiration in many ways, as you'll read in the Block Party participants' own words. As a participant yourself, you'll be asked to try techniques you may feel intimidated by and discover new favorites in the process. You'll get to experiment with color combinations or fabric choices that you wouldn't ordinarily have chosen on your own, and as a result you'll find yourself making discoveries about color that you love.

In the workshops I have been teaching for the last several years, I have found that the best way to really learn something (to understand it viscerally and not just intellectually) is to make it happen with your own hands. Your fellow bee members will deliver invaluable opportunities to creatively challenge yourself, to reach outside your comfortable and familiar habits. By helping your fellow bee members to create their quilt vision, you'll expand your own. Have fun!

Denyse Schmidt

introduction

The Quilting Bee

Since the early nineteenth century, women have been coming together to quilt. Gathering regularly to work together on a quilt, a group of neighbor women would sit around a quilting frame, chatting and enjoying one another's company while completing some productive stitching. These gatherings came to be known as quilting bees. As years passed, the popularity of quilting ebbed and flowed, but through it all many quilters continued to enjoy the community and friendship provided by quilting bees.

As the decades have passed, the lives of women have changed significantly. No longer limited to friends and neighbors, our communities have grown to include the whole wide world we can find online. The Internet has allowed quilters to come together in an entirely new way.

Through the Internet, quilters who live far apart have connected with one another to form a vibrant and active community celebrating the art of modern quilting. Blogs, Flickr groups, message boards—the new generation of quilters has embraced these technologies. We use these tools to find like-minded quilters, to share our work with other members of the community, and to discuss tips and techniques. The Internet is a constant source of inspiration, feedback, and advice. With no geographical limitations, the online community of modern quilters will continue to grow and thrive.

The combination of the traditional craft of quilting and an active online community has given birth to the "virtual" quilting bee.

Three blocks for a hexagon quilt (full quilt on page 83)

WHAT IS A VIRTUAL QUILTING BEE?

A virtual quilting bee is a way for quilters who live far away from each other to come together and collaborate to produce quilts for each member of the bee. Generally, bees have twelve members, one for each month of the year. Each bee member is assigned a month. The bee member assigned a given month mails the eleven other quilters the fabric of her choice, along with suggestions for the style of block she would like the bee members to make. The eleven quilters make the blocks and mail them back to that month's bee member, who then assembles the blocks into the quilt of her choice.

Depending on the initial request, the blocks might vary in size or might all be the same. Assembling the quilt top with the various blocks can be challenging, but it's also a lot of fun. Often the creator of the quilt will have to make choices that push her out of her quilting comfort zone, and this process can lead to unexpected and wonderful results.

Throughout the entire process, all twelve quilters blog about the inspiration for their particular month, the blocks they create, and the quilts they have assembled.

Every bee needs a creator and host. The host is responsible for inviting other quilters to join the bee, for organizing the bee, for setting deadlines,

and for responding to all questions. Anyone can host a bee—all you need is a passion for quilting and a willingness to organize a bee.

For the Block Party bee, co-hosts Alissa and Kristen brought together ten fellow bee members who share a modern quilting aesthetic. Each month, this community of quilters is united by their participation in the sewing of one quilt, yet each individual quilting voice is represented in the finished product.

This modern quilting bee allows the twelve quilters to recapture the sense of community and support experienced by the members of a traditional bee, even though the members live all across the country, or even the world.

We hope this book will inspire you to join in the fun and take part in—or even start—a quilting bee. If you would like to create your own bee, take a look at The Hive Mind: Bee Tips & Suggestions (page 96) for ideas on how to make it a success.

How to Use This Book

This book contains twelve project chapters, one for each month in our year-long quilting bee. Within each chapter, you will find the instructions for the block featured in that month's quilt, photos of the finished quilt, information to help you create your own version, and—just for fun—a little bit about that month's contributor.

You will probably notice that this book is different from other quilting books you have used.

This is because our approach to modern quilting focuses on free piecing and designing as we go, rather than on strict cutting requirements and exacting patterns. Instead of precisely cut pieces, we tend to use scraps that fall within an approximate range of measurements. Similarly, we rarely use templates. For us, quilting is more fun when we do not have to worry about precise piecing and can instead design as we go.

Here's one example of freestyle "wonky" piecing (full quilt on page 38).

Throughout the book, you will see that we use—and promote using—fabric we have on hand, including scraps and found materials such as recycled clothing. Generally, we use fabrics from a variety of fabric lines, rather than pulling all the fabrics for a quilt from a single collection. If you have not yet acquired a sufficient stash, we have included the fabric quantities used in these blocks so that you will be certain to buy enough.

Following the twelve months of quilts, we have included a chapter called Collective Wisdom, in which we share general techniques and tips we have learned and gathered from other bee members. This chapter provides a brief overview of the process for creating a quilt from start to finish. Readers who are new to quilting may find it useful to start by reading through the entire chapter, which covers topics ranging from color pairings and fabric selection to quilt layouts and binding.

This book is designed around our Block Party bee, which means that in each quilt we have blocks created by twelve different quilters. While we encourage everyone to start or join a bee, each quilt featured in our book can be made by a single quilter. Once you have learned the basic process of making a quilt, you can easily mix and match the techniques you have learned to create your own designs.

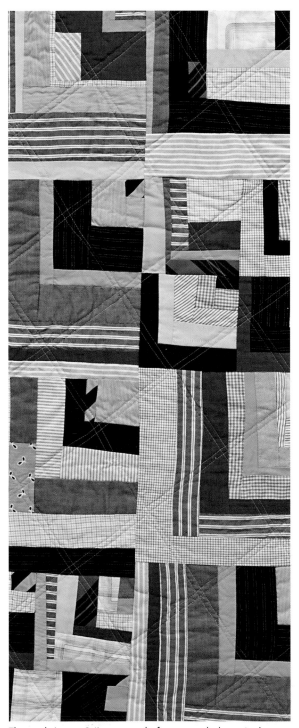

This quilt (page 24) was made from recycled men's shirts.

WONKY LOG CABIN BLOCK

ONCE AROUND THE BLOCK, 95″ × 95″, designed, assembled, and quilted by Alissa Haight Carlton. *Photo by Alissa Haight Carlton*

For the first month of the quilting bee, Alissa sent a mix of patterned and solid fabrics to the other bee members. Her bold color choices of orange, aqua, and gray are a wonderful example of today's fresh, modern color combinations. For more about color, see Modern Color Pairings (page 99). For the block, Alissa chose a "wonky" spin on the traditional Log Cabin block. This wonky block provides a perfect introduction to improvisational, or freestyle, piecing.

Alissa's fabric choices

Wonky Log Cabin Block

Alissa requested that all the bee members make wonky Log Cabin blocks—a variation of the traditional Log Cabin block, which has a center square surrounded by simple strips ("logs") of a variety of fabrics.

TRADITIONAL LOG CABIN BLOCK AND SOME VARIATIONS

This block is a perfect starting point for new quilters. Easy to make, it is loved by quilting novices and experts alike. The Log Cabin block has many variations, making it the perfect canvas for showing off your creativity. This versatile block can be used with all your favorite prints, both large-scale and small-scale. It's also a great scrap-eater, so grab your scrap basket and pull out any coordinating snippets.

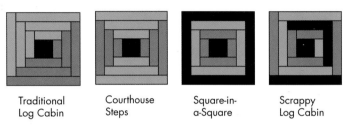

Traditional
Log Cabin

Courthouse
Steps

Square-in-
a-Square

Scrappy
Log Cabin

Log Cabin variations

Follow the diagram for each block to see how the colors play in the construction. The traditional Log Cabin block uses one color for the bottom and right-hand logs, and another color for the top and left-hand logs. In Courthouse Steps, one color is used in the top and bottom logs and another color is used in the left- and right-hand logs. In the Square-in-a-Square block, the center and each round of the block is a distinct color. Last but not least, the scrappy Log Cabin features a mixing and matching of color throughout the rounds.

✳tip: Are you new to quilting and don't have a scrap basket yet? How about finding someone to do a swap with? Maybe you have a yard of fabric that another quilter would trade for a load of her scraps. There are also fabric shops (especially those on etsy.com) that sell scrap packs. Fat quarters—precut 22″ x 18″ pieces sold at quilt shops and online—are also a great way to buy small quantities of fabric so that you can affordably get some variety in your stash.

How to Make a Wonky Log Cabin Block

The general technique for building this block is the same as for the traditional Log Cabin block—round by round. However, instead of straight strips, you use irregularly shaped pieces and add them wherever you like. Your finished block size can vary, depending on how many strips you add. It's up to you!

✳ **tip:** In improvisational piecing, the idea is to cut and piece a quilt block "free-style." There is no need to precisely measure and cut all the strips. Instead, you cut free-hand and use your creativity to figure out the arrangement of shapes and colors that is most pleasing to you. There is no right or wrong way to do it, and improvisational piecing is freeing and fun. You can take this approach to making almost any quilt block.

FABRICS AND CONSTRUCTION

Alissa asked each bee member to make 2 blocks between 14″ × 14″ and 17″ × 17″. Alissa planned to later frame the blocks to make them 19″ × 19″ when finished. She cut 8 yards of different solid and print fabrics into 6″ × 22″ strips and also added some scraps of coordinating fabrics from her stash. She sent a varied selection of 10 fabric strips to each member. This was more than enough fabric for the bee members to make 2 blocks each.

Fabrics

For your own blocks, you will need a variety of fabric scraps. If you have lots of strips of fabric that are randomly cut and varying in size (width and length), you are all set. Make sure you include some that are long enough to be the final logs of your blocks, 14″ to 17″ long.

For each block, you will need to have a center (of any size) and 10 to 15 strips about 4″ wide and of varying lengths, which you will chop up as you are making the block. The number of different fabrics you use completely depends on your fabric and design choices.

Construction

Makes 1 block the size of your choice.

1. Build on the center of the block, log by log, working counterclockwise. Don't worry about cutting perfect strips—just cut and sew what you think looks good. Also keep in mind that you can add "wonk" to your block by trimming a strip on an angle after it has been sewn on.

2. Continue building on the block, round by round, adding logs in a counterclockwise direction and pressing after each addition. Add as many rounds to the block as you'd like, picking and placing fabrics in the manner you find attractive. Stop adding rounds once the block has reached the desired dimensions. Trim the edges of the block, squaring it up using the grid on your cutting mat and a rotary cutter and ruler. For help with this, see Squaring Up Fabric (page 106).

tip: As you construct your blocks, try to put contrasting fabrics next to one another—mix up the prints you are using. Consider both pattern and scale. You might also want to vary the width of the strips for interest.

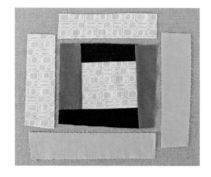 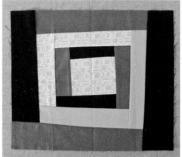

Variations

In making these blocks, feel free to be creative and put your own spin on things. The almost limitless options can result in a wide variety of different finished looks. Consider building one log out of multiple fabrics, as Kristen did in one of the blocks she made for Alissa. Or, add multiple logs to one side before sewing one onto the top, as Alissa did. Build the center out of different fabrics. Jacquie did just that and showed off the center by framing it with dark gray.

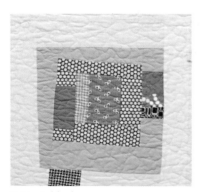

Kristen's block

Jacquie's block

Alissa's block

ALISSA'S QUILT:
Once Around the Block

The wonderful wonky blocks Alissa received from the bee members resulted in a bold, lively, and dynamic quilt.

LAYOUT

To learn about different layouts, see Quilt Top Layouts (page 108).

This finished quilt has 25 blocks. Because the blocks were irregular sizes, she added frames to make the finished blocks all the same size. Alissa chose an off-white fabric to showcase each block individually and to unify the quilt top. After framing, she trimmed each block to measure 19½" square. See Framing Blocks (page 109) for more information.

From 4¼ yards of background fabric, Alissa cut 100 strips 3" × 20" for framing the blocks. This gave her extra-large strips, making it easy to just sew them on and trim afterward.

✳tip: Because the bee members contributed blocks in a variety of sizes, Alissa had to trim down some of the framed blocks significantly to reach the finished size of 19½" square. For other blocks, the framing strips hardly needed any trimming at all.

Alissa sewed the framed blocks together in a 5 × 5 grid to create a finished quilt measuring 95" × 95". This large quilt works nicely on a queen-size bed, adding warmth and color to Alissa's bedroom.

FINISHING

For general finishing information, including layering, backing, quilting, and binding, see Collective Wisdom (pages 98–126).

Alissa chose to back her quilt by stitching together 3 sections of fabric in her 3 main solid colors—gray, aqua, and orange. She made her design choices just by working with the fabric she had remaining from the quilt blocks and some solid off-white. She quilted the quilt on her home sewing machine, using an allover stippled design, and bound it with a gray print fabric also found in the blocks. Altogether, Alissa needed 8⅔ yards of fabric for her backing, and she needed ⅞ yard for the binding.

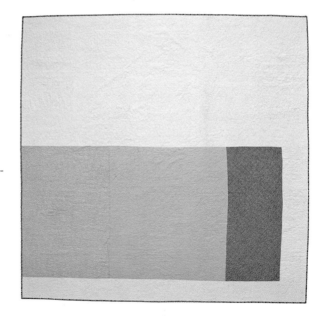

ALISSA'S THOUGHTS ON THE QUILTING BEE

I started quilting just four years ago, and it was my exposure to various Internet communities that helped to get me hooked. When Kristen and I started the bee, I thought it would be a wonderful way to create a community of friends who quilt. When I joined the bee I did not have any "real life" friends who quilt, so getting to know these eleven women through the blocks they sewed has been wonderful!

I was surprised to learn that being in the bee made me a better quilter. Working with fabrics and design requests that other people chose pushed me to be creative and attempt new techniques that I wouldn't otherwise have tried.

All the quilts that resulted from the bee are amazing! And even better, I now know a group of women who love quilting, and modern quilts, as much as I do.

Alissa Haight Carlton lives in Los Angeles with her filmmaker husband. She has been obsessively quilting for four years. She is one of the founders of the Modern Quilt Guild. When not quilting, she casts reality TV shows, including seasons seven and eight of Project Runway. *She blogs about her quilting at www.handmadebyalissa.com.*

Photo by Gavin Carlton

2
february
QUARTERED LOG CABIN BLOCK

SQUARE DEAL, 50″ x 50″, designed, assembled, and quilted by Nettie Peterson. *Photo by Nettie Peterson*

For February, Nettie turned to a wonderful source of fabric: upcycled men's shirts and neckties. With a cool palette of blue and a splash of warm yellow, this cozy quilt makes the perfect play mat for Nettie's beautiful children. To read more about fabrics, both new and upcycled, see Selecting Fabrics (page 101). She chose a Quartered Log Cabin block, which takes a Square-in-a-Square Log Cabin block and cuts it in quarters to create four smaller blocks. The resulting wonky blocks are graphic and fun.

Nettie's fabric choices

How to Make a Wonky Quartered Log Cabin Block

For this block, you construct a Square-in-a-Square version of the Log Cabin block (page 14). Then you chop up the block in quarters to make 4 smaller blocks and reassemble them into a new block.

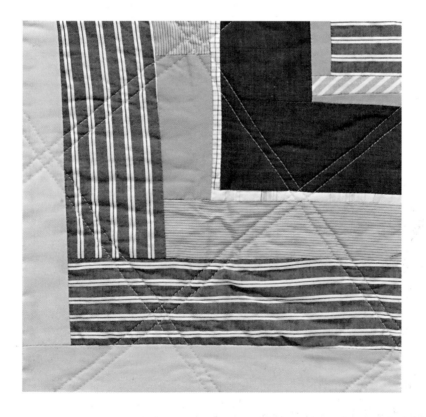

FABRICS AND CONSTRUCTION

For her blocks, Nettie cut up 12 men's shirts that she found at a thrift store. She sent each bee member 6 pieces of a shirt (a sleeve, a front half, or half of a back), with each person receiving pieces from 6 different shirts. She also sent along some scraps from 2 neckties. To create additional interest, she cut 2 half-yards of solid quilting cottons each into 12 strips 3″ × 22″ and included them too.

To create an eye-catching look, Nettie wanted different-sized blocks to work with when putting her quilt together. She requested that some bee members make 21″ × 21″ blocks that when cut in quarters would be 10½″ × 10½″ (10″ square finished), and that others make 11″ × 11″ blocks that would become 5½″ × 5½″ quarter-blocks (5″ square finished).

Fabrics

For your own blocks, you will need at least 2 shirts per block, but the more shirts you have, the more variety you can include in all the blocks. For 1 block, you'll need a center (any size you would like) and 12 to 20 long strips of shirts that are a variety of widths from 1½″ to 4″. Some of the strips must be at least 22″ long for the last rounds of the largest squares.

Construction

Makes finished blocks 10″ × 10″.

If you're planning on making all the squares in your quilt yourself, make 5 of them 21″ square and 5 of them 11″ square so that you'll have a mix of sizes to work with when you're ready to determine the layout. The 21″ squares will be cut into quarters to make 20 blocks. The smaller squares will be cut into quarters and reassembled to make 5 blocks.

1. For the Square-in-a-Square variation of the Log Cabin block, the same fabric is used for all the logs in a single complete round. Cut a fabric square the size of your choice for the block center. To make a Square-in-a-Square block for this quilt, sew 2 side logs to the center first and trim. Then add the top and bottom logs and trim. This creates a square look that works particularly well when cut into quarters.

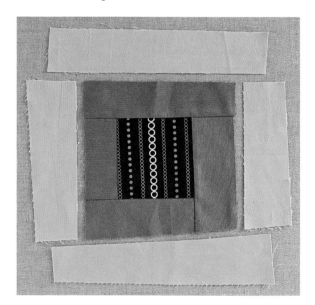

2. Continue sewing on strips as in Step 1, adding enough rounds to make either a 22″ square or a 12″ square. Remember to press each seam along the way. Once the blocks are big enough, square up each to 21″ or 11″ square.

3. Cut each square in equal quarters to create 4 blocks 10½″ × 10½″ (from a 21″ square) or 4 squares 5½″ × 5½″ (from an 11″ square). Set the 10½″ blocks aside.

4. With the 5½″ quarters, reassemble the pieces to make 10½″ unfinished blocks. You can arrange them into any layout you like. One way is to combine 4 mismatched quarters into a new Square-in-a-Square. Alternatively, you can keep the quarters all pointing the same way, which creates a very different but equally interesting block.

NETTIE'S QUILT: **Square Deal**

Including pops of yellow among all these blues gives this quilt a wonderful, vibrant look. Even though she had the bee members use men's shirts that she bought for about $2 each at her local thrift store, the quilt is beautiful. What an economical way to make an amazing quilt!

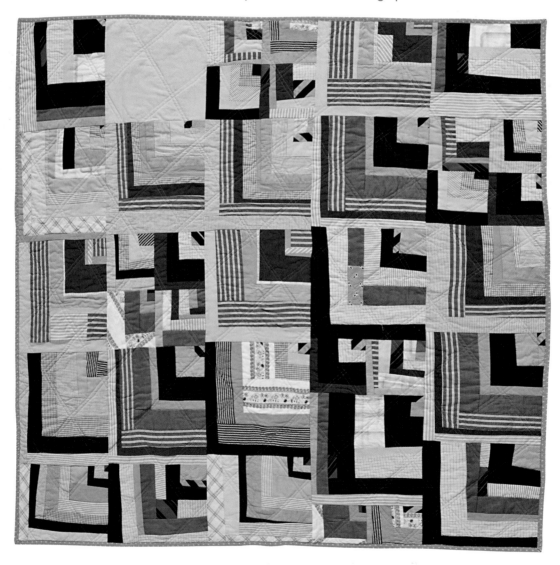

LAYOUT

To learn about different layouts, see Quilt Top Layouts (page 108).

Rather than looking at this quilt as horizontal rows, Nettie arranged the blocks in 5 columns. The first column has 5 large blocks. She threw in a solid block at the top of column 2 and then added 4 blocks. Column 3 is again 5 blocks, but in column 4 she used 4 blocks and 2 half blocks. The last column has 5 blocks again. She then sewed the columns to each other to make a 50″ × 50″ finished quilt.

FINISHING

For general finishing information, including layering, backing, quilting, and binding, see Collective Wisdom (pages 98–126).

Nettie backed her quilt with some additional blocks from her quilt top, combined with plain, pale blue fabric. Her quilt is straight-line machine quilted in a diagonal grid pattern. She added a binding of green dotted fabric. For a one-fabric back, Nettie need 3¼ yards of fabric and ½ yard for the binding.

NETTIE'S THOUGHTS ON THE QUILTING BEE

I started quilting about ten years ago. My co-worker was a quilter, and she shared the most beautiful quilts I had ever seen. I knew how to sew a straight line, and I figured I'd give it a try. It didn't take long before I was hooked.

Eventually my husband and I moved away (and I started having babies), and I found that I missed my friendships with my quilting/sewing friends. That's when I discovered the wonderful world of online quilting!

You never know what people will ask you to make for them—the thought of hexagons scared me to death, but they ended up being my favorite block. I also discovered some methods that I do not really prefer (paper piecing), but I'm glad I gave it a try and that I know how to do it. This bee has also taught me that I do my best work when I do not overthink things. If I sit down at my sewing machine and just sew, I tend to like the results better than when I try to plan them out.

Most importantly, I have found friends in this bee. The generosity and kindness of the members is by far the best part of being involved in a quilting bee. I love that I have a quilt made up of blocks from all over the country, and from all different types of quilters. I think we all consider ourselves modern quilters, but I can definitely see everyone's different style come out in her blocks. Thanks, ladies.

Nettie Peterson lives in Denver, Colorado, with her husband and three children, with whom she stays home. In addition to quilting, she enjoys photography, gardening, bike rides, the outdoors, thunderstorms, and being with her family. She blogs at http://aquiltisnice.blogspot.com.

Photo by Nettie Peterson

march

WONKY NINE-PATCH BLOCK

WHOLE NINE YARDS, 70½" × 82", designed, assembled, and quilted by Ashley Shannon. *Photo by Ashley Shannon*

Ashley's fabric choices

For March, Ashley requested a fresh, bright quilt to curl up under while she waited for spring. She requested that modern meet traditional with this wonky twist on a very well-known traditional quilt block—the Nine-Patch block. The great floral fabrics reminiscent of vintage sheets contribute to the wonderful combination of a modern design sensibility with a hint of tradition thrown in.

A Nine-Patch block itself is very traditional, but depending on the fabric patterns and color choices, the block can take on a new look. Add some wonkiness and it's contemporary!

Traditional Nine-Patch Blocks

Scrappy
Nine-Patch

Two fabric
Nine-Patch

White/print
Nine-Patch

Nine-Patch variations

The Nine-Patch block is a common beginner's block in traditional quilting. It's so easy to make—it's just nine squares of fabric sewn together in a grid. As a scrappy block, with nine different print fabrics, the block has a free and funky feel. By adding a contrasting solid to a mix of fabric prints, you give the block a balanced, graphic look. And using white, the popular look of the 1930s that has come full circle, the design looks completely modern to our twenty-first-century tastes. The high contrast of two colors allows this block to look lively but not too busy.

How to Make the Wonky Nine-Patch Block

Ashley chose the 2-color option for her blocks, but she wanted some playful modern wonkiness added as well. This method of making wonky Nine-Patch blocks is fun, quick, and incredibly simple.

FABRICS AND CONSTRUCTION

Ashley wanted to use 10 different fabrics, and she needed 42 blocks for the quilt she planned to make. She cut out 4 squares 12″ × 12″ from 8 of the fabrics, and 5 squares 12″ × 12″ from the remaining 2 fabrics, for a total of 42 squares. To the bee members, she sent out a total of 21 pairs of 12″ fabric squares. Some bee members received 1 pair to make 2 blocks, and others received 2 pairs to make 4 blocks. With a block this quick, easy, and fun, having a bee member to make 4 blocks is not asking too much.

Ashley's block choice was both striking and economical. It's a good block to ask for if you don't want to send large amounts of fabric to other bee members. For 10″ finished blocks you can send precut 12″ squares to people, and very little fabric goes to waste.

Fabrics

To make 2 blocks 10″ × 10″ finished in 2 fabrics, you will need a 12″ square of each fabric. About ¾ yard each of all 10 fabrics is enough to make 42 blocks this size with fabric left over for your stash.

If you want a different size for the Nine-Patch block, just determine the desired finished block size, then add 2″ to it. For example, if you want a finished 15″ block, start with 2 fabric squares 17″ × 17″.

Construction

Makes 2 finished 10″ × 10″ blocks.

1. Stack 2 contrasting 12″ squares with right sides facing up.

2. Use a rotary cutter and a ruler to cut them into 9 wonky pieces by cutting 2 rows and 2 columns. Do not be scared of wonk! Embrace it. Make those lines crooked and off-kilter.

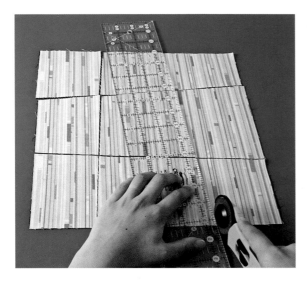

3. Separate the 2 sets of pieces, laying them out next to each other with the pieces in their original positions. Lay out the "new" blocks by trading the fabric pieces between blocks but keeping the pieces in their corresponding locations.

4. Sew a block together by sewing the pieces into rows, pressing, and then sewing the rows to each other and pressing again. Trim the block to a 10½″ × 10½″ square. Repeat for the second block. You now have 2 wonky Nine-Patch blocks!

*tip: You can use this same method to make scrappy Nine-Patch blocks with nine different fabrics. If you stack and cut nine fabrics at once, you can then alternate around all the fabrics to make up nine different blocks—each block will have all nine fabrics in it. To cut the stack of nine fabrics, make sure your rotary cutter blade is nice and sharp, as you're pushing the limits of how many layers of fabric you can cut at once!

ASHLEY'S QUILT:

Whole Nine Yards

Ashley's quilt has ten different fabrics in it, all combined in pairs, creating a fun and modern twist on a very traditional pattern.

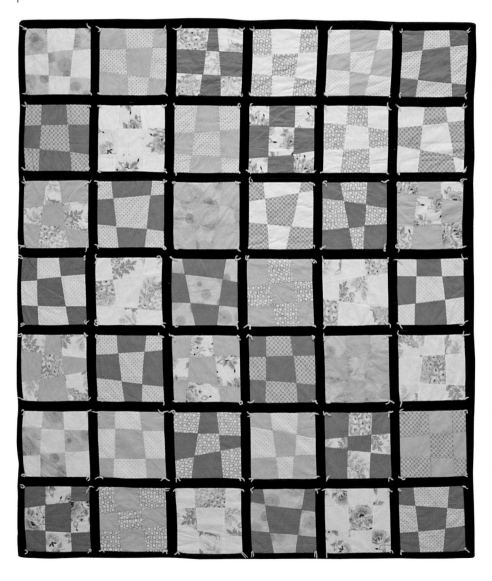

LAYOUT

To learn about different layouts, see Quilt Top Layouts (page 108).

For her quilt layout, Ashley chose a 6 × 7 grid with sashing. For the sashing, she chose a deep navy solid that provides a lovely contrast to the white, soft green, and light blue block fabrics.

She used 2 yards of fabric for the sashing. Accurate measuring and cutting is essential to use sashing successfully.

She cut 8 strips 2″ × 71″ lengthwise for the long horizontal sashing between the rows and for the top and bottom of the quilt. She then cut 49 strips 2″ × 10½″ for the short vertical sashing between the blocks and for the ends of each row. She sewed the blocks and sashing into rows and pressed the rows. Then she joined the long sashing pieces and the rows together.

FINISHING

For general finishing information, including layering, backing, quilting, and binding, see Collective Wisdom (pages 98–126).

Ashley used the same navy solid fabric in the backing and binding and pieced the back with fabrics from the blocks. (For a one-fabric back, Ashley would need have needed 5 yards of fabric and ⅝ yard for the binding.) Instead of quilting the top, she chose the quick and simple method of tying it with yarn. For more about this method, see Quilting (page 115).

Her 42 finished 10″ blocks with 1½″ finished sashing created a 71″ × 82″ finished quilt.

Photo by Ashley Shannon

ASHLEY'S THOUGHTS ON THE QUILTING BEE

In 2005, I moved to Michigan from Austin, Texas. Austin is a crafter's mecca—people there do everything from fabric design to embroidery to knitting to sewing. So in my move, not only did I lose warm weather and breakfast tacos, I lost the sense of being among people who could share in the joy of creating beautiful, useful things. Lucky for me, then, that I moved when I did: at the moment when craft blogs and websites were really hitting their stride, opening up a whole new way for me to find communities of people to connect with.

The Block Party quilting bee meets an important need in my life: It allows me to connect with, learn from, and be inspired by a group of women from around the country. And it reinvigorates my desire to be a maker of beautiful things. In making blocks for the quilts in this book, I had to try techniques I probably would not have investigated on my own, but that made me a better quilter; I had to explore color palettes that I would never have chosen on my own, but that allowed me to see colors in new and inspirational ways. My own quilt, with crisp navy setting off fresh greens and whites, evokes summer picnics and naps on rolling lawns; its wonky nine-patch construction is straightforward yet engagingly offbeat. Best of all, it is the tangible manifestation of the quilting bee spirit: individual contributions working together to create a cheerful, lovely whole. It is a virtual community embodied, and a perfect reminder that I am never alone in my love of crafting!

Ashley Shannon is a professor of nineteenth-century British literature. She lives in Grand Rapids, Michigan, where she shares an apartment with biggish stashes of yarn and fabric and a smallish mutt named Bailey.

april

WONKY TRIANGLES BLOCK

FALLING TO PIECES, 61″ x 73″, designed, assembled, and quilted by Ashley Newcomb.

Ashley's fabric choices

Ashley's wonky triangle blocks lead to a distinctive and lively quilt. The grays, blues, purples, and greens evoke the flowers and budding trees of spring. Although triangles can sometimes be tough to work with, these free-pieced blocks are fun and simple to sew up. Working with triangles is always a great way to practice piecing, a key quiltmaking skill.

Basic Half-Square Triangles

Half-square triangles can be arranged in many ways, and they serve as the foundation of many blocks, both traditional and modern. If you haven't made the traditional version before, you might want to try it before embarking on making our wonky version. Be aware, though, that traditional half-square triangles require consistent ¼″ seams to maintain the triangle points at every seam. Find information online about traditional half-square triangles, and you'll discover several different methods for sewing them.

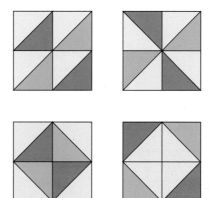

Some traditional half-square triangle block layouts, including pinwheels, diamonds, and zigzags

How to Make the Wonky Triangles Block

This block creates a different and funky look with a variety of triangle sizes and shapes using our free-piecing method. Consistent ¼″ seams are not crucial, but seams should never be less than ¼″.

tip: If you want to use more wonky half-square triangles in your block, cut more rectangles from the original background piece, but remember to allow ½″ for seam allowances per additional row or column. Also, the orientation of all the bias edges should be the same within a block, but it can vary from block to block.

- -

FABRICS AND CONSTRUCTION

For her blocks, Ashley chose a lively mix of 15 different patterned and solid fabrics for the triangles and a charcoal gray for the background. From 3 yards of fabric, she sent each bee member a fat quarter (a precut 18″ × 22″ piece) of the background fabric and a variety of 12 squares 6″ × 6″ for the triangles.

Construction

Makes 1 finished 15″ × 12″ block.

1. From the background fabric, cut an 18″ × 14″ rectangle. Cut this rectangle into rows and columns. (Don't wonk these cuts.) This example shows 12 rectangle pieces of 4 columns and 3 rows on the cutting mat.

2. From a scrap square, cut a triangle to sew to the first of the 12 rectangles. As shown, 2 sides of the triangle should be longer than the sides of the rectangle. You will trim off the extra later. Always err on the side of cutting bigger triangles; it's easier to trim them down than to tear them out and start over!

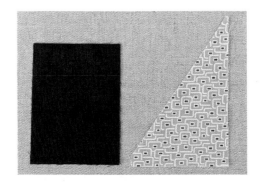

3. Position the triangle on the background, with right sides together, so the triangle's bias edge is diagonal on the background. Sew the bias edge of the triangle to the rectangle. The diagonal doesn't have to be from corner to corner on the background piece. Mix up the triangle sizes to provide variety in your block.

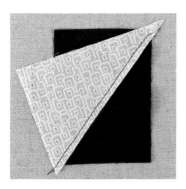

4. Trim off the excess rectangle fabric, leaving at least a ¼″ seam allowance, and press the triangle away from the background.

5. Now trim only the excess triangle fabric to create a rectangle.

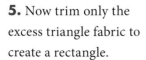

6. Repeat Steps 2–5 until you have made all 12 triangles for your block. Make sure all of your triangles are facing the same direction. Arrange rectangles into 3 rows of 4.

7. Sew together the 3 rows of triangles, using a ¼″ seam allowance, and press. Sew the rows to each other and press. Square up the block to 15½″ × 12½″ and you have a completed block.

ASHLEY'S QUILT:

Falling to Pieces

This unique layout that Ashley designed for her quilt really showcases the blocks the bee members made for her. She used some beautiful gray and blue solids to frame groups of three blocks. The one backward block (technically a mistake!) contributes additional interest to the quilt.

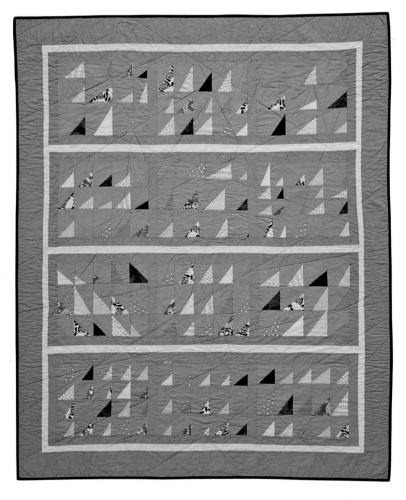

*tip: Sometimes a "mistake" in a quilt can lead to the quilt's most interesting design aspect. Embrace the idea of making changes and shifts in your quilts as you go along. Perfection can be boring! The organic nature of creating a quilt may include missteps that lead to a more beautiful quilt than you could ever have planned.

LAYOUT

To learn about different layouts, see Quilt Top Layouts (page 108).

When Ashley got her blocks back, she arranged the blocks into 4 rows of 3 blocks each, with a gray 1½″ finished sashing strip between the blocks. Then she sewed the blocks into rows, framed each row with a gray 1½″ finished frame, and added a finished 1″ light blue sashing between rows. She added an inside finished 1″ border of light blue, and a gray outside border that finished at 4″. The finished quilt measures 61″ × 73″.

It takes 1⅞ yards of fabric for the gray sashing, frames, and outside border, and ⅝ yard of the light blue fabric to assemble the quilt in this style.

FINISHING

For general finishing information, including layering, backing, quilting, and binding, see Collective Wisdom (pages 98–126).

Ashley pieced together an interesting backing that's mostly gray background fabric but features a section pieced from leftover triangle fabrics. If Ashley had used a single fabric for her backing, she would have needed 3⅞ yards of fabric and ⅝ yard for the binding. The quilt is machine quilted in a random pattern of diagonal lines and is bound in solid dark blue.

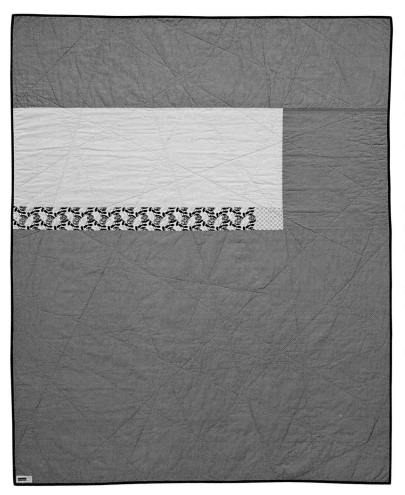

ASHLEY'S THOUGHTS ON THE QUILTING BEE

This quilting bee has been such fun! My absolute favorite part is that it gives me the ability to connect with other like-minded quilters. Ironically, some of these quilters were the very same people who actually inspired me to start quilting. My interest was initially sparked not by taking a quilting class but by spending hours looking at photos of modern quilts online. The more I looked, the more I wanted to quilt. And then I discovered virtual quilting bees.

Each month I am challenged to do something I may not have done or thought of on my own. For instance, I always steered clear of hand sewing. And English paper piecing? No, thank you! But after Rashida requested it for her month and I gave it a try, I discovered that not only is it fun, it is also really addictive!

I feel so honored to be a part of this group and to have the chance to collaborate with so many fabulously talented quilters. There's something really fun about contributing little pieces to their quilts—and something very special about having them contribute to mine. The unique perspectives and techniques that each person in this group brings to a similar stack of fabric never ceases to amaze me.

And most of all, I love looking at my finished quilt and being able to say that these blocks were made by some of my favorite quilters!

Ashley Newcomb lives in Vermont with her husband of two years. Her day job is in finance, but her passion is for her newly discovered hobbies of quilting and fabric collecting. Ashley can often be found with camera in hand looking for new locations to photograph her quilts. She blogs and shares these photos online at www.filminthefridge.com.

Photo by Morgan Newcomb

may

STRING X BLOCK

X MARKS THE SPOT, 48″ × 48″, designed, assembled, and quilted by Josie Stott.

Josie's fabric choices

Josie's May blocks have lovely texture and depth due to the combination of gorgeous natural linen and the warm tones of quilting cottons. The String X block that she requested is a variation of an old favorite, the String quilt. This scrappy block is made with a quick and simple variation of foundation paper piecing. In this quilt, the many tiny little scraps are easier to manage with paper support, and the paper makes it really easy to sew on the right size scraps without measuring them beforehand.

For each block, you will create a wonky pieced strip from small scraps of assorted fabrics. Then you will sew the strip between two triangles of the solid background fabric. The pattern these blocks create doesn't develop until the all blocks are assembled to form bold, bright X's, giving the finished quilt a much greater impact than that of each individual block.

Foundation Paper Piecing

Foundation paper piecing is most often used to make complex and detailed shapes because— when done properly—it produces perfectly accurate blocks every time. However, there is no "drawing outside the lines" in this type of paper piecing, so we modern quilters are not prone to do much of it. Although we enjoy complex blocks, we prefer to let our own creativity shine.

In traditional foundation paper piecing, you trace or print out a template of shapes on paper. Following the numerical order on the template, you place fabric pieces on the back side of the printed paper, and from the front of the template you stitch exactly on the lines indicated on the paper template. You stitch the fabric pieces to each other and to the paper at the same time. You trim seam allowances as you go. When the block is complete, you tear off the paper. (The machine stitching has perforated it, making it easier to tear out; still, be gentle so you don't rip out the stitches.) For more information on paper piecing, you can find entire books on the subject at your local quilt shop; use the Internet as an additional resource.

With foundation piecing, a thin foundation such as lightweight muslin may sometimes be used instead of paper. This is a better choice for people who find it very tedious to tear out the paper foundation after stitching. The drawback of using fabric as the foundation is that the finished block will be a bit bulkier with the extra background layer of fabric. Why not try both methods to discover which you prefer?

*tip: Although quilters often use special foundation paper for piecing, you can use scrap paper for this project. It is a great way to use up those computer printouts that you don't need, but first test the printed paper to make sure that neither steam nor heat will cause the ink to transfer to your fabric or ironing board cover. It's always smart to reuse when you can in quilting and in life.

How to Make the String X Block

This is a fun and easy construction method that uses strips. We have paper pieced the strips, but these same steps will also work with a fabric foundation. With our method, you use a gluestick to attach small strips of fabric to a strip of paper.

FABRICS AND CONSTRUCTION

From 2 yards of 42″-wide natural linen, Josie sent each bee member an 11″ × 11″ square. She also sent everyone 6″ × 6″ squares of 9 different coordinating fabrics—3 solids and 6 prints—in warm reds and browns. So that she would have 16 blocks, Josie asked 4 people to make 2 blocks and everyone else made 1 block.

Fabrics

For 1 block you will need an 11″ × 11″ square of the background fabric and a decent handful of scraps that are at least 4½″ wide by 1″ to 3″ long. You can control how wonky you make the piecing by how you place the fabric as you sew it down.

Construction

Makes 1 finished 12″ × 12″ block.

1. Cut out a strip of foundation paper 4″ × 18″. With a gluestick, attach the first piece of fabric at one end of the paper. Be sure you just use a basic gluestick for paper and nothing that will make it hard to pull the paper from the fabric.

2. Set your sewing machine stitch length to a very short stitch. This means the needle perforations will be close together as you sew, making it easy to remove the paper later.

3. Place a second piece of fabric on top of the first, right sides together, and sew the pieces together along the bottom edge as shown. You can sew a straight seam or an angled seam. In fact, the more angled you sew, the more wonky your piecing will look.

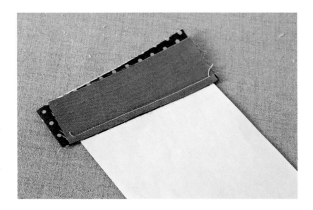

4. Swipe a bit of glue on the next section of paper and fold down the second piece of fabric, finger-pressing it firmly onto the glued surface. If you run your fingernail along the seam, it will lie flat. Continue stitching and gluing fabrics until you have covered the entire strip of paper.

5. Flip over the fabric-covered paper and trim off the excess fabric along the paper edges, using a ruler and rotary cutter. You have now finished a pretty strip of piecing!

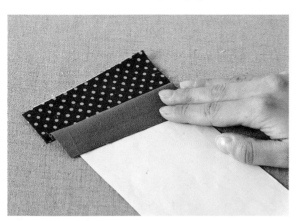

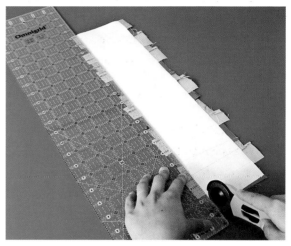

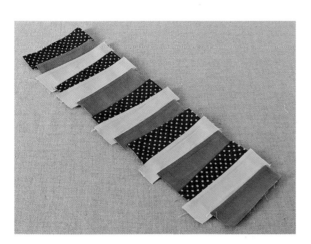

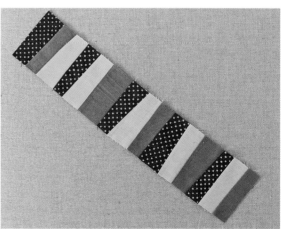

6. Carefully tear off the paper from the back of the strip. This is where you will be happy you set your stitch length to very short! If you used a fabric foundation, you can skip this step.

7. Cut the 11″ square of background fabric diagonally from corner to corner to create 2 right triangles.

8. Align the strip between the 2 triangles so that the block will be as square as possible. Sew the triangles to either side of the strip.

✳tip: You'll be working with big triangles that have a long bias edge. That edge is easy to stretch, so handle the triangles carefully. Don't tug, pull, or stretch the fabric at all as you work with it.

9. Using a ruler and rotary cutter, square up the block to a perfect 12½″ × 12½″. You now have a finished block! Make 3 more and you will see the X pattern that these fun blocks create.

✳tip: Many quilting and sewing stores carry square 12½″ × 12½″ rulers. This ruler is not vital to making your block square, but it can make the cutting process super easy.

X Marks the Spot

In Josie's quilt, the linen mixed with the warm color palette of reds and browns created a quilt that was classic, yet still youthful.

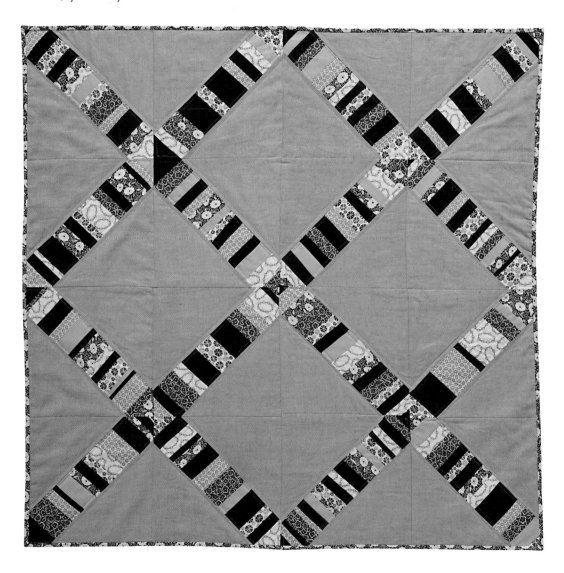

LAYOUT

To learn about different layouts, see Quilt Top Layouts (page 108).

Each of Josie's finished blocks measured 12″ × 12″ when all sewn up. She arranged her 16 blocks in 4 rows of 4 blocks, carefully matching the points of all of the X's. Josie's finished quilt measures 48″ × 48″, a size perfectly suited for a baby quilt or small throw.

FINISHING

For general finishing information, including layering, backing, quilting, and binding, see Collective Wisdom (pages 98–126).

Josie's quilt is backed in solid, deep red with a single pieced strip running through it. She needed 3¼ yards of the backing fabric and ½ yard for the binding. She chose to lightly quilt her quilt, just quilting along the X's, and bound it in a small-scale print from the blocks.

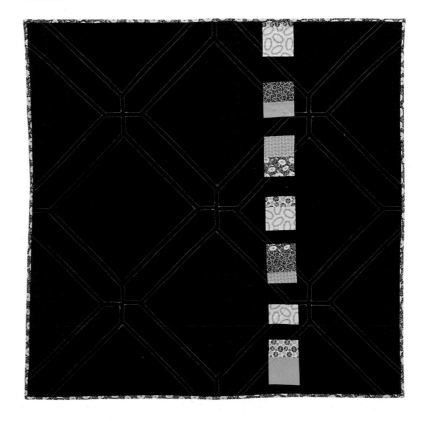

Photo by Josie Stott

JOSIE'S THOUGHTS ON THE QUILTING BEE

The bee has been an all-around great experience for me, but the winning element has been all the snack-size opportunities. I loved that each month I got the chance to try out a new technique, a new fabric, and a new color combination—and my only commitment to it was a block or two. I encountered many quilt blocks throughout the bee that I'd wanted to try beforehand, but the prospect of making a whole quilt of them had been too daunting.

The same applies for color and fabrics. Each participant has such a unique and wonderful eye for color that opening each package and completing the blocks was a real pleasure. I received combinations of fabric I would never have thought to put together and marveled at how beautiful they looked. I experimented with new techniques such as raw-edge appliqué, and I even completed my first-ever Dresden Plate.

As I finished the bee I realized that my own quilting had developed so much. I have a new set of skills, new color palettes, and new-found confidence. Having the chance to try fabric and sewing ideas in bite-size portions was like being at a quilting tapas bar. Pure joy.

Josie Stott lives in Brooklyn, New York, with her husband and two kids. She has been quilting for six years and crafting for as long as she can remember. She blogs about her crafty adventures at www.breadandbuttons.blogspot.com.

june

WONKY ROMAN STRIPE BLOCK

SLIDING BY, 90″ × 90″, designed and assembled by Kristen Lejnieks, quilted by the Artful Quilter in Burke, Virginia. *Photo by Kristen Lejnieks*

For June, Kristen chose a sophisticated palette of taupes and grays with pops of citron and aqua. Although not made with typical summer colors, this quilt looks destined for afternoons at the beach, picnics at the park, and lounging outside on long summer days. Kristen's chosen block is an update on the traditional Roman Stripe block. The wonky stripes and bold triangles are a perfect complement to warm neutrals, subtle prints, and pops of color.

Kristen's fabric choices

Traditional Roman Stripe Block

A traditional Roman Stripe block has strips of equal width sewn parallel to the long edge of a right triangle.

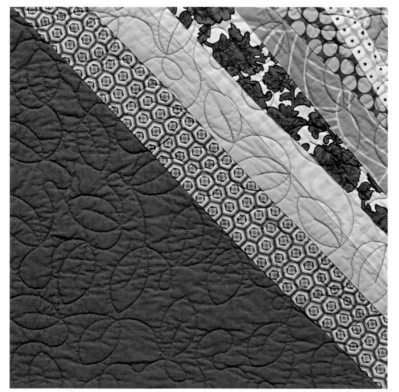

With wonky piecing, you have more flexibility and room for creativity. You can mix strips of different widths and vary the angles in your piecing.

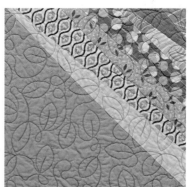

Strips of different widths and angles

How to Make a Wonky Roman Stripe Block

This wonky block is constructed in the same basic manner as a traditional Roman Stripe block, except that the strips vary in width and are cut on an angle or curved. A simple paper template makes it easy to trim the block evenly after piecing.

FABRICS AND CONSTRUCTION

Kristen asked each bee member to make 3 blocks and sent each bee member 2 squares 17½″ × 17½″ of background fabric, plus 7 to 10 strips of contrasting fabrics of various widths and lengths, both prints and solids, for each block. (Keep in mind that each background square makes 2 blocks.) Although it may seem like a lot to ask, these blocks are very easy and come together very quickly.

Fabrics

For this block, you will need a fat quarter of the solid background fabric, as well as strips of 8 to 10 different contrasting print and solid fabrics (in total approximately ½ yard). The strips can be anywhere from 1″ to 4″ wide. They can vary in length, but the longest strips should be at least 24″ long.

You can make this block any size. As a rule of thumb, always start with a square of fabric that is at least 2½″ bigger than the desired finished block size. For example, Kristen wanted to make a 15″ × 15″ finished block, so she started with a square of fabric at least 17½″ × 17½″.

Construction

Makes 1 finished 15″ × 15″ block.

1. Cut the 17½″ square of background fabric diagonally from corner to corner to create 2 right triangles. Set 1 triangle aside; you will need only 1 triangle per block.

2. Cut a template from freezer paper the same size as the unfinished block—in this case, 15½″ × 15½″. Crease it along a diagonal, from corner to corner, and set it aside.

✳tip: You can use any large paper to create the template, but we like freezer paper from the grocery store because you can iron the shiny side of the freezer paper to the block at the end. When you trim, the template stays in place. No slipping, and you wind up with accurate blocks!

3. Sew the longest strip to the long edge of the triangle. Be gentle with the bias edge of the triangle. Continue adding strips in increasingly shorter lengths. As you add new strips, vary the colors and patterns in a pleasing way. For example, try to mix solids and patterns. Also avoid placing 2 strips of similar colors right next to each other. Press the seams when you have added enough strips to complete your block.

background fabric and the first strip meet. Iron the shiny side of the freezer paper to the front of the block.

4. As you add strips, check the growing block against the paper template to ensure that the strips are long enough.

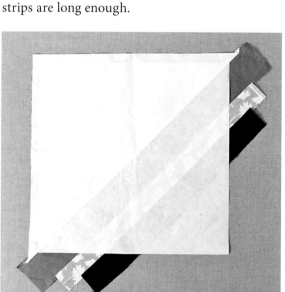

5. Add strips until you have enough to completely cover the template. Center the diagonal crease over the block's center, that is, where the

6. Use a ruler and rotary cutter to trim the excess fabric along the template edges, and then peel off the freezer paper. You can use this template 3 or 4 times before needing another one.

Sliding By

Kristen's strips of citron-green and aqua pop against the various background neutral fabrics, creating a graphic statement.

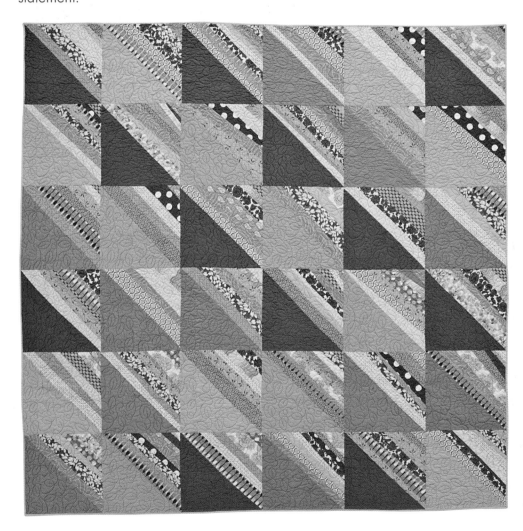

LAYOUT

To learn about different layouts, see Quilt Top Layouts (page 108).

Kristen chose to lay out her blocks in 6 rows of 6 blocks each. She arranged all the triangles facing the same direction, which gives this block a graphic and modern feel. This layout of blocks is the simplest of all—just blocks. You sew the blocks directly to one another in rows and then the rows to each other. This layout works well for geometric blocks, which often form a pleasing pattern when adjacent to each other, as you can see in this quilt.

With 15″ blocks, the quilt finishes at 90″ × 90″, which is large enough for a queen bed.

FINISHING

For general finishing information, including layering, backing, quilting, and binding, see Collective Wisdom (pages 98–126).

Kristen sent her quilt to a longarm quilter, who quilted a beautiful allover leaf pattern. The quilt is bound in the same solid chartreuse green fabric found in the blocks, which pops against the neutral background fabric. The back of Kristen's quilt features a large-scale bird print and incorporates both the neutrals and the prints featured on the quilt top. For a one-fabric backing, Kristen would have used 8¼ yards of fabric, and she needed ⅞ yard for the binding.

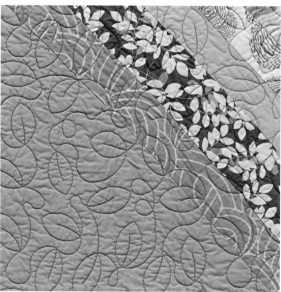

KRISTEN'S THOUGHTS ON THE QUILTING BEE

For a long time, I didn't even realize that there was a modern quilting movement because I didn't know a single other modern quilter. My local fabric stores featured few modern quilting fabrics, leading me to order almost all my fabric online. I sewed alone. I shared my projects and fabric purchases with my friends and family.

Finally I joined Flickr, and this opened up a whole new world to me. I met the nicest, kindest, and most generous group of people who shared my love of nontraditional quilting. After seeing a number of quilting bees online, I finally got up the courage to email Alissa (a Flickr friend) and ask her if she might, just maybe, possibly be interested in running a bee with me. Finally, I had found a quilting home—a group of people to share with and collaborate with!

For me, the bee has been all about making those connections that I wasn't able to make in "real" life. Because of the Internet and the bee, I now have plenty of quilting friends all over the country. So, although my family and friends may not care about my new Flea Market Fancy purchase or my fabulous thrift-store fabric find, I have eleven new friends who do. And I can't wait to tell them all about it.

Kristen Lejnieks is an attorney currently living in Washington, D.C., with her husband and two daughters (ages two and three). She loves to bite off more than she can chew, whether it be starting a quilt three days before a baby shower or agreeing to write a book while working full-time. Kristen blogs (sporadically) at www.kristenunraveled.com.

Photo by Kristen Lejnieks

july

MODERN DRESDEN PLATE BLOCK

PROFIT MARGINS, 72″ x 90″, designed and assembled by Jacquie Gering, and quilted by Angela Walters.

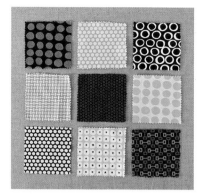

Jacquie's fabric choices

Jacquie's bright and funky Dresden Plates make for a bold, summery quilt that evokes the good times of backyard barbecues and summer fun. When they heard her request, some of the bee members were a tad squeamish about tackling this block. It involves appliqué, a seemingly challenging technique in which fabric shapes are cut out and stitched to the background by machine or by hand. But with each other's support, the bee members all overcame their fears. For general information about various appliqué methods, see Appliqué (page 108).

This whimsical spin on a traditional block resulted in a truly beautiful quilt. The aqua and red color scheme, combined with the small-scale patterned fabric, perfectly complements this block.

How to Make a Modern Dresden Plate Block

The technique we present for making this block is traditional, but the fabric choices and block setting give it a modern look. The bee members all appliquéd their circular "plates" to the block backgrounds using a machine zigzag stitch.

FABRICS AND CONSTRUCTION

Jacquie sent each quilter a batch of 20 rectangles 3″ × 6″ for cutting the wedges. She did some pre-planning to make sure that there was a mix of red and aqua print fabrics in each batch. She also sent each person a 5″ × 5″ square of polka dot fabric for the center and a 16″ × 16″ square of solid white background fabric.

Fabrics

For your own blocks, you will need a variety of (anywhere from 5 to 20) fabric scraps for the wedges, a 5″ × 5″ square for the center, and a 16″ × 16″ square of background fabric. You will also need a 5″ × 5″ square of lightweight interfacing, which you will use to turn under the edges of the center circle.

Construction

Makes 1 finished 15″ × 15″ block.

Templates are on page 64. Note that seam allowances are included for both the wedge and the circle.

1. Use a copy machine to copy the templates (page 64). Cut out the templates. Use the wedge template to carefully cut 20 wedges from the print fabrics. Be sure to select a good mix of fabrics.

tip: Make a durable plastic version of the template by simply cutting it out of a sheet of acrylic plastic that you can buy at most craft stores. Do not use your fabric rotary cutter or fabric scissors when cutting the plastic.

----

2. Join the wedges into a circle by sewing accurate ¼″ seams along the long edges of the wedges. Take care to sew straight, even seams so that you will have a nice round circle of wedges. Press the seams in one direction around the circle.

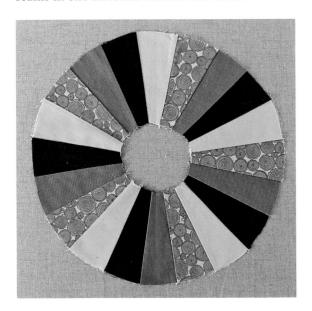

3. Machine stitch around the outer edge of the wedges, a scant ¼″ from the edge.

4. Press under the outside edge, using the stitching line as a guide. If needed, pin the outside edge in place so that it doesn't move as you press. (If your pins have plastic heads, be careful not to melt them!)

5. Pin the wedge circle to the background square, centering it on the square, and appliqué (page 108) the circle to the background. On this block we used a machine zigzag stitch, but you don't have to. You can machine sew it on with a straight stitch or even sew it by hand. If you do zigzag stitch, take care that the zigzag overlaps the circle edge to the background fabric. Set your stitch to a medium width.

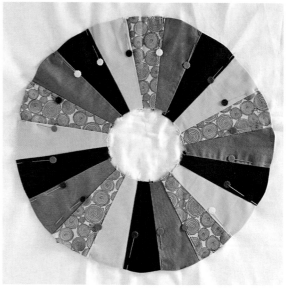

✳**tip:** When you pin the wedge circle to the background, place a pin first on one side and then on the opposite side of the circle, and work your way around, alternating sides as you go.

6. Using the center circle template, cut out 1 piece from the center fabric and 1 piece of interfacing. Place the interfacing and the right side of the center circle together and sew completely around the edge using an even ¼″ seam allowance.

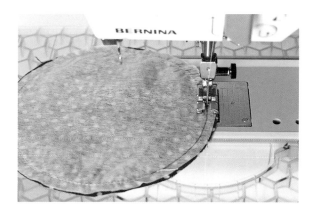

7. Cut a small slit in the middle of the interfacing only and turn the center right side out.

8. Press the center and pin it to the block.

9. Appliqué the circle as the block center—again using the appliqué method of your choice. Trim the block to 15½″ × 15½″ square.

Profit Margins

Jacquie wanted a modern spin on the traditional Dresden Plate block. She asked the bee members to group the red and blue fabrics together and to make sure each block had a variety of each color grouping. This created a graphic pie-chart look that made the design fresh and not in the least like a traditional Dresden Plate quilt.

LAYOUT

To learn about different layouts, see Quilt Top Layouts (page 108).

Before assembling her quilt, Jacquie framed all the blocks. Her blocks have wonky frames in red and blue polka dot print fabrics (from the same print, but in 2 colorways), but 3 of the blocks have solid red wonky frames. Jacquie sewed strips about 5″ wide to the sides of the blocks. She then squared up the blocks to 18½″ × 18½″, with the center of the block rotated at the angle that she liked (pages 109–110). This angle created the wonky frame for each block.

Jacquie's blocks finished at 18″ × 18″. Jacquie arranged her quilt in 5 rows of 4 blocks each, resulting in a 72″ × 90″ quilt.

FINISHING

For general finishing information, including layering, backing, quilting, and binding, see Collective Wisdom (pages 98–126).

Jacquie made a traditional single-fabric backing using a red print fabric. She used 5½ yards for the back and ¾ yard for the binding. The quilt is longarm machine quilted in a wonderful swirl pattern, and the binding is solid red.

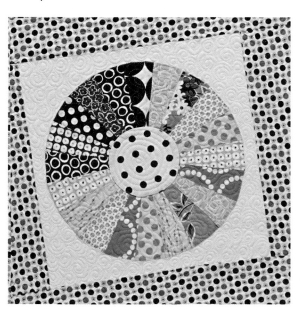

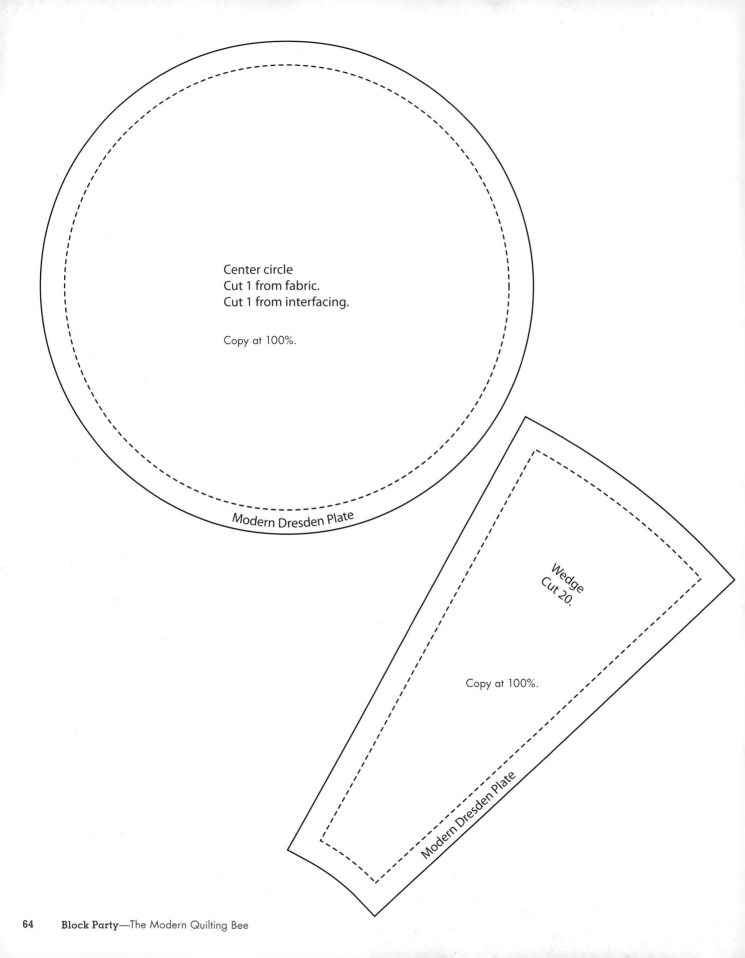

Center circle
Cut 1 from fabric.
Cut 1 from interfacing.

Copy at 100%.

Modern Dresden Plate

Wedge
Cut 20.

Copy at 100%.

Modern Dresden Plate

Photo by Jacquie Gering

JACQUIE'S THOUGHTS ON THE QUILTING BEE

All during the year, I loved those days when my walk to the mailbox was rewarded with a little brown envelope filled with fabric. They were filled with challenges that allowed me to flex my creative muscles—opportunities to make blocks or use techniques I had never used before, or a chance to work with fabric combinations that were out of my comfort zone. They were filled with possibilities. Possibilities are why I joined the Block Party virtual quilting bee.

For me there's always a touch of anxiety when I spread out the fabric and read the instructions. Making blocks for others pushes me to do my best for someone else. Sometimes I dive right in to making the blocks and sometimes I take time to consider my options, but every time as I start sewing the anxiety fades and excitement takes over.

And then there are the days when those little brown envelopes are filled with completed blocks from the other bee members, and block by block a quilt begins to take shape. It's always surprising to see how my bee buddies combine my fabrics and what techniques they use to make the blocks. The finished quilt is a true collaborative effort.

As we've worked together, I've formed virtual friendships with many of my fellow bee members. Someday we may even meet for real. It's possible.

Jacquie Gering lives with her husband, Steve, and her black lab, Bruno, on 110 acres in northeast Kansas. Jacquie discovered quilting as a creative outlet 3 years ago, though she has been sewing most of her life. Jacquie has moved on from more than 25 years in education to full-time quilting. She teaches improvisational quiltmaking in her studio, designs and makes quilts, and blogs about quilting and her life at www.tallgrassprairiestudio.blogspot.com.

august

POLKA DOT BLOCK

CONNECT THE DOTS, 74" × 67", designed, assembled, and quilted by Lisa Billings. *Photo by Lisa Billings*

For August, Lisa chose an array of bright, cheerful colors, including fuchsia, orange, purple, and bright pink. She asked the bee members to use the appliqué method of their choice to create a large block with a field of scattered polka dots. (For information about appliqué techniques, see Appliqué, page 108.) The combination of the joyful polka dots and happy colors makes this the perfect summer quilt. Using large blocks means that this quilt comes together quickly, even with only twelve blocks, and the spray of dots allows for a wide variety of patterns.

Lisa's fabric choices

How to Make a Polka Dot Block

FABRICS AND CONSTRUCTION

Lisa chose a solid charcoal background fabric to set off the bright orange, fuchsia, and pink fabrics she selected for the polka dots. She had 3 yards of fabric for the background. For each block, she sent the bee members a fat quarter of the charcoal fabric, as well as 8 squares 7″ × 7″ of solid and patterned fabric for the dots. For your own blocks, you can use scraps of fabrics from your stash for the polka dots or you can choose a few coordinating fat quarters.

For Lisa's quilt, the bee members used a variety of appliqué methods (page 108), including fused appliqué, needle-turn appliqué, and turned-edge appliqué.

Fabrics

You'll need a 17½″ × 21½″ background rectangle and scraps of various prints for the circles. You will also need some lightweight fusible web.

Construction

Makes 1 finished 17″ × 21″ block, using the fused appliqué method.

1. Trim the background fabric to 17½″ × 21½″.

2. Follow the manufacturer's instructions for the fusible web to apply the web to the fabric pieces you are using for the circles. Leave the paper backing on the web.

3. Using a pencil or washable fabric marker, mark circles of various sizes on the paper backing of the fusible web. You can use a compass to make the circles, or raid your kitchen cabinets and use bowls, cups, mugs, and wineglasses as templates. With the fused appliqué method, no seam allowance is needed.

4. Cut out the circles and arrange them on the background fabric in a pleasing way. Mix sizes and fabrics, and overlap or cluster them in interesting arrangements. Fuse the circles to the background according to the manufacturer's instructions. Then use a small zigzag stitch around the edge of the circles. This ensures that the circles will stay put after machine washing.

Connect the Dots

This playful arrangement of circles in each block gives the
illusion of bright-colored balloons dancing across the quilt.

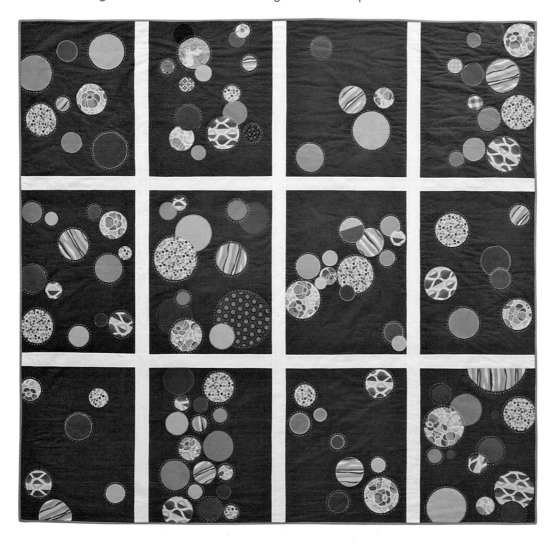

LAYOUT

To learn about different layouts, see Quilt Top Layouts (page 108).

Each quilter made 1 block 17″ × 21″ for Lisa. Lisa arranged the 12 blocks in 3 rows of 4 blocks each, adding 2″-wide finished sashing in a clean, neutral ivory. Lisa's quilt finished at 74″ × 67″. When you use sashing, be sure to carefully measure and trim the blocks to size, and to accurately measure and cut the sashing strip width and length for a straight quilt top.

FINISHING

For general finishing information, including layering, backing, quilting, and binding, see Collective Wisdom (pages 98–126).

Lisa backed her quilt with large sections of fabric in 2 shades of pink. She used 4¼ yards of fabric for the backing and ⅝ yard for the binding. She hand quilted around many polka dots using white thread for contrast, and left the background unquilted. She bound the quilt in a bright pink solid, playing off the pink in the patterned polka dots.

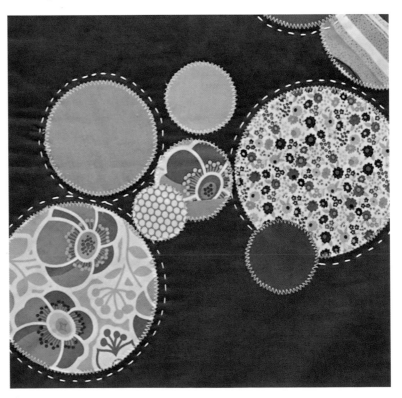

LISA'S THOUGHTS ON THE QUILTING BEE

Participating in this quilting bee was exciting and challenging. Waiting for a new package of fabrics each month got my creative juices flowing. I looked forward to going onto the blog, learning new techniques, and seeing the other bee members' inspiration. I would sometimes receive fabrics that were not necessarily "me," but once the block was constructed I always loved it. This was my favorite aspect of the bee, and as a result I have a whole new palette of inspiration that I will incorporate into future quilts.

Overall, this has been one of the most rewarding and creative experiences of my life. When spotting my blocks in the finished quilts, I feel as though these treasured objects have a bit of me in them. The modern quilting style and improvisational techniques have expanded my skill set. More than anything, though, participating in the bee has enabled me to connect with other quilters across the country who share my passion for quilting.

Lisa Billings lives outside Providence, Rhode Island, with Jeff, her husband of sixteen years; Olivia, her daughter; and her wacky cat, Violet. She started quilting about fifteen years ago and is thrilled with how quilting has really taken off in such a modern and exciting direction. Besides quilting, she loves to experience the Providence cultural scene, cook (and eat!), and keep up with her etsy shop (www.pinklemonadeboutique.etsy.com), where she sells her handbags.

Photo by Olivia Billings

september

UNEVEN COINS BLOCK

HEADS OR TAILS, 36″ × 60″, designed, assembled, and quilted by Sarah Johnson.

Sometimes called Stacked Coins or Chinese Coins, coin quilts have become popular among modern quilters, and for good reason. They showcase today's graphic prints and come together quickly and easily. The traditional coin quilt pattern features straight vertical strips of uniformly cut fabric rectangles set into a solid background. Sarah's quilt provides a different take on this favorite pattern by varying the size and position of the coins. Sarah chose a neutral warm brown as her background color, with the primary fabrics a range of chartreuse, grass green, aqua, and teal prints.

Sarah's fabric choices

How to Make an Uneven Coins Block

Although you can use this technique to create any size of block, Sarah asked the bee members to create finished 12″ × 15″ blocks.

TRADITIONAL COIN BLOCK

Traditional
Chinese Coins

FABRIC AND CONSTRUCTION

For each block, Sarah sent a fat quarter of chocolate brown background fabric (for a total of 3 yards of background fabric) and between 8 and 15 strips of contrasting fabrics. The strips were anywhere from 3″ to 8″ long and varied between 1″ and 3″ wide.

Construction

Makes 1 finished 12″ × 15″ block.

1. Cut the fat quarter of background fabric into strips 18″ long. Vary the width of the strips from 1″ to 3″. Cut the strips in half, so that you have strips 9″ long.

2. Sew contrasting strips between background strips as shown. Choose background strips close in width to the print scrap. Press.

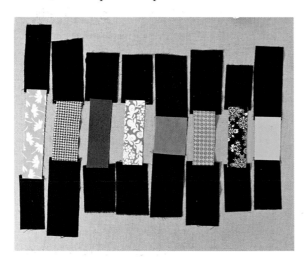

3. Trim the strips so the long edges are even and straight. If you wish, you can trim the strips at a slight angle, which will add wonkiness to the finished block.

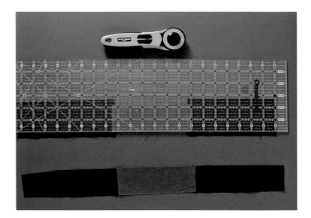

4. Sew the strips together along the long edges to create stacks, varying the position of the print fabrics. When you have added sufficient strips to create a block 16″ tall, press all the seams. Trim the block to 12½″ × 15½″.

Heads or Tails

Sarah, a librarian, loves how this block evokes stacks of beautifully bound books—a teetering column in someone's personal collection. In other colorways, this block might suggest piles of flat stones or even a child's tower of blocks.

LAYOUT

To learn about different layouts, see Quilt Top Layouts (page 108).

Each bee member created 1 block for Sarah, who sewed the 12 blocks together into 3 columns. Her quilt finished at 36″ × 60″—perfect for her new baby to snuggle underneath as the autumn nights grew cool and the days grow shorter. Notice how the top corner blocks don't have "books" stacked to the top.

FINISHING

For general finishing information, including layering, backing, quilting, and binding, see Collective Wisdom (pages 98–126).

Sarah used 2 yards of brown fabric for a simple single-fabric backing for her quilt and machine quilted horizontal lines across the "stacks." She used ½ yard to bind the quilt in brown to match the background, creating a uniform ground for the stacks of coins.

SARAH'S THOUGHTS ON THE QUILTING BEE

Connecting with other quilters isn't the easiest thing for a modern-day girl. In the days of old, women gathered together for quilting bees, helping each other to share in a common experience through work and community. While there are many who still gather in person for bees today, many of us who otherwise would be kindred spirits are separated by great distances, especially those of us with a flair for the more modern.

When I was asked to join Block Party, I was thrilled to be able to get to know not only new quilting styles and techniques, but also eleven other women who inspired me each month as we became friends through our blocks. The online community of crafters holds a wealth of experience, ideas, and beauty and is a world where creativity and encouragement abound!

Sarah Johnson lives in Chicago with her husband and son, dreaming of the day they'll move to the woods. She loves to quilt, read, cook, sew, and explore. Sarah blogs about quilting and life at http://sarahlookingin. blogspot.com.

Photo by Hauna Ondrey

HEXAGON BLOCK

SPECKS OF HEX, 54˝ × 60˝, designed, assembled, and quilted by Rashida Coleman-Hale. *Photo by Rashida Coleman-Hale*

Rashida's fabric choices

For October, Rashida requested a smattering of hand-pieced hexagons in a classic red, yellow, and royal blue color scheme. The bright colors perfectly complemented this geometric block.

The hexagon has been used by generations of quilters. Most commonly, hexagons are hand sewn using paper templates and basting stitches. Many modern quilters have rediscovered the hexagon. The simplicity and portability of the hexagon units have made it a new favorite.

Traditional English Paper Piecing

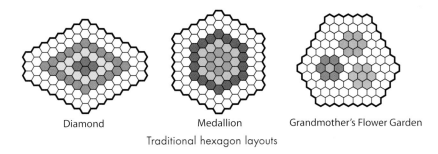

Diamond   Medallion   Grandmother's Flower Garden

Traditional hexagon layouts

Traditionally, hexagon quilts are laid out in patterns that utilize hexagons of uniform size.

Hexagons are made with traditional English paper piecing. In this technique, you use paper templates and hand sewing to create perfectly formed hexagons. The process may look a little intimidating, but once you get the hang of it, hexagons come together quickly and easily. After making the individual hexagons, you can join them directly to one another to create different patterns.

You will need a paper template for each hexagon you want to make. You can copy the templates in this book, print hexagons from various sources online, or order precut paper pieces in bulk from a quilting website.

On page 84, we have included templates for both 2½″ and 1¼″ hexagons, which finish at 5″ and 2½″ across, respectively. When referring to the size of the hexagon, it equals the length of one of its six sides. For the 2½″ hexagon, start with a 5½″ × 5½″ square of fabric. For the 1¼″ hexagon, start with a 3¼″ × 3¼″ square of fabric.

MAKING A HEXAGON

Makes 1 finished 2½″ hexagon.

1. Cut out a paper copy of the 2½″ template (page 84). You will need a paper template for each hexagon that you make.

2. Cut a 5½″ square of fabric. Place the template on the wrong side of the fabric square. Pin the paper hexagon onto the fabric, keeping it centered.

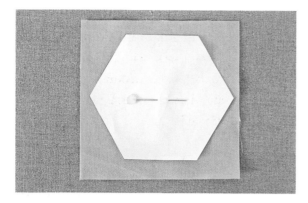

3. Fold a corner of the square over a side of the paper hexagon. While holding the corner against the paper, fold the edge of the fabric square over an adjacent side of the hexagon.

4. On the back of the hexagon (with the paper facing you), make a couple of small stitches to secure the fold at the corner of the hexagon. Do not knot the basting thread, but leave a 2″ to 3″ tail of thread as you start basting. When you stitch, catch the layers of fabric but be sure not to sew the paper. This will make it easier to remove the paper later.

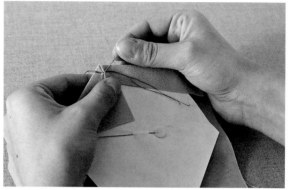

5. Work your way around the hexagon, folding the square of fabric down against the edge of the paper and basting at the corners. Keep the fabric folded right up against the edges of the paper as you work. After you have basted all 6 corners, leave another 2″ to 3″ tail of thread. Press the finished hexagon, but leave the paper in for now.

JOINING HEXAGONS

Hexagons can be joined directly to one another.

1. With the paper still inside, place 2 hexagons right sides together, matching the corners. With a needle and thread, whipstitch the 2 pieces together along an edge. Try to catch only a few threads on each edge, and do not sew through the paper.

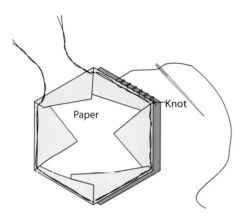

2. Continue sewing pieces to each other in the same way. Once the edges of the hexagon are sewn to the surrounding pieces, pull out the paper. Even if you have accidentally caught the edge of the paper with your thread, it will usually pull free with a slight tug.

3. Press the assembled hexagons. Because the basting stitches are only on the back of the hexagons, they can be left in.

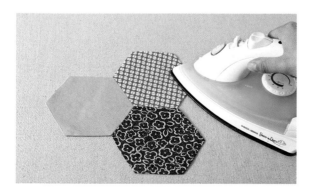

How to Make a Scattered Hex Block

For her modern spin on this block, Rashida wanted random scatterings of colorful hexagons in 2 sizes on a white background. This modern twist is both beautiful and practical, as these scattered hexes require fewer hand-sewn hexagons than the traditional layout.

FABRICS AND CONSTRUCTION

Hexagons are a great way to use small amounts of fabrics from your stash. For this block, Rashida sent each bee member a 15½″ × 18½″ piece from 3 yards of white background fabric, along with 6 different print fabrics between 4″ × 4″ square and 10″ × 10″ square.

Construction

Makes 1 finished 15″ × 18″ block.

1. Using the 2 hexagon templates (page 84), create as many hexagons as you wish.

2. Arrange the hexagons in a pleasing manner on the background fabric, and connect them into groupings using a whipstitch. Remove the paper.

3. Appliqué (page 108) the hexagons to the background fabric using your favorite technique. We have sewn the hexagons onto the background fabric using a machine straight stitch approximately ¼″ from the edge of the hexagon.

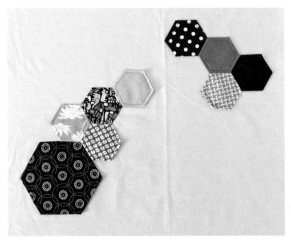

Here are some favorites from Rashida's quilt:

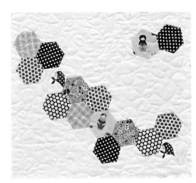

Ashley's block

Kristen's block

Alissa's block

RASHIDA'S QUILT:

Specks of Hex

Each bee member created a scattered hexagon block for
Rashida. These blocks all contain elements of traditional
hexagon patterns but look utterly modern strewn across the
white background.

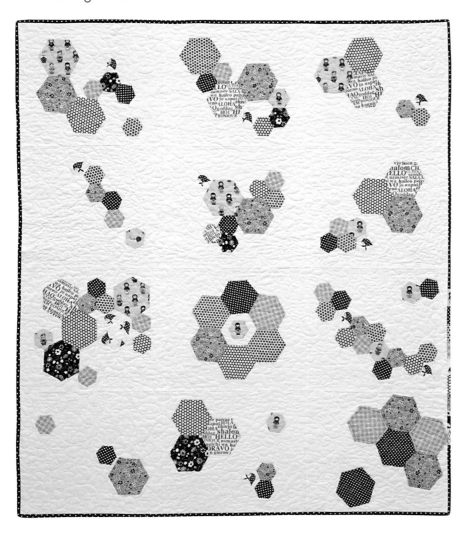

LAYOUT

To learn about different layouts, see Quilt Top Layouts (page 108).

Rashida chose to arrange her 12 blocks a 3 × 4 layout, and her finished quilt measures 54″ × 60″. By joining the blocks directly to each other, Rashida emphasized the negative space. The complex arrangements of hexagons remind us of the molecule diagrams from chemistry class—organic and beautiful.

FINISHING

For general finishing information, including layering, backing, quilting, and binding, see Collective Wisdom (pages 98–126).

Rashida used extra hexagons on the quilt back, arranging them in a long vertical column, using 3½ yards of white fabric. Her quilt is machine quilted in a stippled pattern and bound from ½ yard of red dot fabric with a small section of binding made from mixed fabrics.

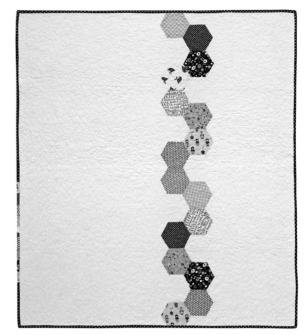

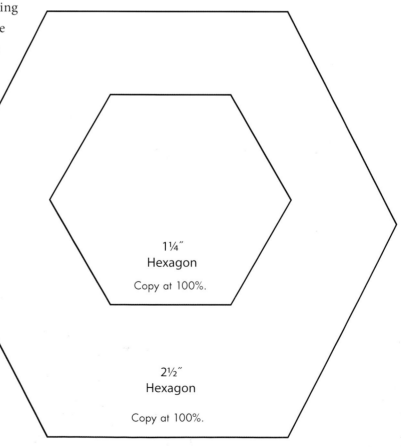

1¼″
Hexagon

Copy at 100%.

2½″
Hexagon

Copy at 100%.

RASHIDA'S THOUGHTS ON THE QUILTING BEE

I have been in love with the concept of joining creative forces with the members of a group to design one gorgeous quilt! Learning some new sewing tricks along the way is also an awesome bonus. It's been so much fun to receive a package once a month filled with a delightful array of fabric pretties ready to be made into something special. It can be a bit of a challenge to create a block with colors, fabric, and design criteria that aren't your own, but I think it helped to push me creatively and got me to think outside the box a little.

We are all at different skill levels and we all have different styles, but that did not matter. The results of our little design collective have been amazing! Participating in Block Party has been a wonderful experience, and I'm so thrilled that I had the opportunity to work with such a talented group of women from all around the country.

Rashida Coleman-Hale studied fashion design at the Fashion Institute of Technology and rediscovered her love of sewing when she became a stay-at-home mom. Her first book, I Love Patchwork, *was released in 2009. She currently lives in Atlanta with her husband and three children. Read more about her crafty life at iheartlinen.typepad.com.*

Photo by Rashida Coleman-Hale

WONKY STRIPE BLOCK

EARN YOUR STRIPES, 60″ × 60″, designed, assembled, and quilted by Elizabeth Hartman.

For her November quilt, Elizabeth chose a vibrant mix of red, coral, orange, gold, and chocolate brown fabrics. She asked each bee member to create a strip of stripes, showcasing the fun mix of solids, dots, and animal prints. The 25 blocks come together in an eye-catching throw, perfect for adding a splash of warm color to her home.

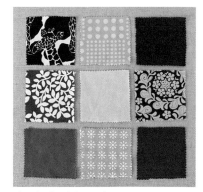

Elizabeth's fabric choices

How to Make a Wonky Stripe Block

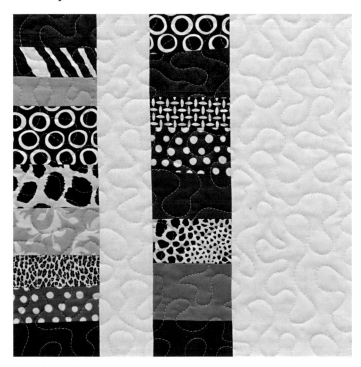

These blocks can have a single strip or 2 strips. The strips can vary in width for a wonky look.

FABRICS AND CONSTRUCTION

For each block, Elizabeth sent 2 pieces of 14″ × 14″ white background fabric, as well as small pieces of fabric in coordinating prints and solids for the strips. She used a total of 3 yards of background fabric. Elizabeth made 3 blocks and had the other bee members each make 2 blocks.

Fabrics

This block is a great scrap-eater and can use up some of those itty-bitty scraps that you can't bear to get rid of.

Construction

Makes 1 finished 12″ × 12″ block with 1 striped strip.

1. Use a rotary cutter and an acrylic ruler to cut the 14″ background square into 2 rectangles. Cut the scrappy fabrics into rectangles that are at least 3½″ wide and vary in height.

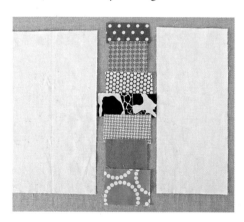

2. Sew the center strips together into a strip that is at least 14″ long.

3. Trim the edges of the pieced strip unit so that they are straight and parallel.

4. Sew the pieced strip unit between the white background pieces. Trim the block to 12½″ × 12½″.

5. To add variety to the quilt, you can also make blocks with 2 pieced strip units. The scrappy strips can be wider or narrower. For a block with 2 pieced strip units, cut the background block into 3 rectangles. Assemble the block as described above, making sure to leave at least 1 edge of the block white. Strips can also be placed to make some vertical stripes in the block center.

Two strips   Some vertical strips

ELIZABETH'S QUILT:
Earn Your Stripes

The bold colors and patterns are set off by the simple white background of the Stripe blocks in Elizabeth's quilt.

LAYOUT

To learn about different layouts, see Quilt Top Layouts (page 108).

Elizabeth had a total of 25 blocks. She arranged these in a 5 × 5 grid and assembled the blocks without sashing or borders—just blocks. Elizabeth's finished quilt measures 60″ × 60″, a perfectly sized throw.

FINISHING

For general finishing information, including layering, backing, quilting, and binding, see Collective Wisdom (pages 98–126).

Elizabeth made a simple 2-fabric backing for her quilt using bright red and orange fabrics. She needed 3⅞ yards of fabric total for her two-fabric back and ⅝ yard for her binding. Using her home sewing machine, she quilted a stippled pattern over the entire quilt and then added a binding of crisp dark brown.

ELIZABETH'S THOUGHTS ON THE QUILTING BEE

For me, the most fun aspect of bees is being challenged to make blocks that fit in with someone else's quilting vision. Each month of a bee brings a new quilter's fabric choices and piecing concepts, which I find refreshing. I like to think of each month's block as a problem to be solved. I love seeing the solutions that all the other members come up with and, of course, the truly fantastic quilts that result from this collaboration.

I also think it is wonderful to get to know the other quilters a little better. Like a lot of us who read and write quilting blogs, I'm used to seeing other people's work online—almost exclusively online. It is so much more exciting to be able to actually hold someone else's work in your hands and be able to make it a part of a project of your own!

Elizabeth Hartman is a self-taught sewer who has been making quilts for about ten years. She lives in Portland, Oregon, and recently quit her longtime corporate job to concentrate on creative projects. Elizabeth's book The Practical Guide to Patchwork: New Basics for the Modern Quiltmaker, *from Stash Books of C&T Publishing, came out in 2010. Elizabeth blogs at www.ohfransson.com.*

Photo by Chris Hartman

CONFETTI BLOCK

PARTY OF TWELVE, 62" × 77", designed, assembled, and quilted by Megan Risse. *Photo by Megan Risse*

Megan's fabric choices

December is all about family, friends, and celebrations, and what is more celebratory than confetti? With its sprinkling of colors and patterns, a quilt like Megan's will add a cheerful splash of color to your home and remind you of the delight and joyfulness at the heart of the holidays.

These freestyle confetti blocks start with snippets of fabrics around which you sew strips of solid background fabric. Blocks can have as many colors and as many snippets as you like—you decide!

How to Make a Confetti Block

These blocks can be made in any size. Megan requested blocks finishing at 13″ × 13″. The blocks contain fabric scraps in different colors and sizes that vary from block to block. Some of Megan's have 6 snippets and some have 16.

FABRICS AND CONSTRUCTION

From 3 yards of fabric, Megan sent each bee member a fat quarter of white background fabric, as well as 8 to 12 scraps ranging in size from 1½″ × 1½″ to 6″ × 6″. She asked bee members to also pull fabric from their own scrap bin.

Construction

Makes 1 finished 13″ × 13″ block.

1. Cut the background fabric into strips, varying from 1″ to 4″ wide and 18″ long. Cut the scraps into rectangles of varying sizes, for example, 2″ × 3″ or 1½″ × 4″.

2. Using the background strips, frame each scrap rectangle by adding strips around the center, as in the Square-in-a-Square (page 22). Trim and press as you go.

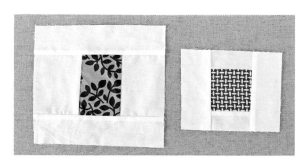

3. Once all the scraps are bordered in the background fabric, lay them all out. Try to fit the framed scraps together like puzzle pieces. Join sections together by adding additional framed units and background strips if needed to make the sections fit together. Square up the units as necessary and press all the seams.

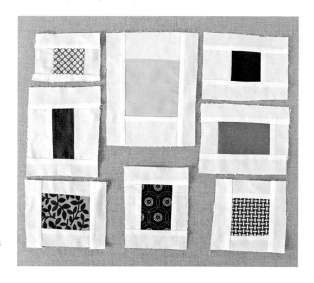

4. Continue sewing the units together until you have a block at least 14″ × 14″ and trim the block to a 13½″ × 13½″ square.

MEGAN'S QUILT:
Party of Twelve

With the blocks all assembled, the specks of confetti have been tossed at a celebration, creating an exciting quilt.

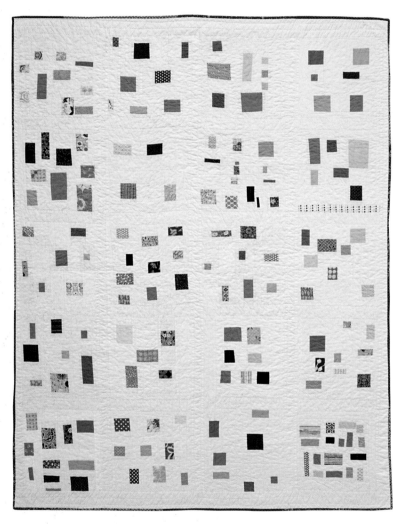

LAYOUT

To learn about different layouts, see Quilt Top Layouts (page 108).

Megan received 20 blocks that finished at 13″ × 13″ and decided to use 2″-finished sashing between all the blocks. The 2½″ sashing strips were cut from the same white fabric as the background. After sewing the blocks together in a 4 × 5 grid with the sashing, Megan added a 2″-finished matching border, making her final quilt a generous 62″ × 77″.

FINISHING

For general finishing information, including layering, backing, quilting, and binding, see Collective Wisdom (pages 98–126).

Megan's quilt has a plain white backing and is machine quilted in an allover stippled pattern. She used 4¾ yards of fabric for the backing and ⅝ yard for the binding. The dark pink binding provides a striking contrast to the white background and complements the many colors of the quilt top.

MEGAN'S THOUGHTS ON THE QUILTING BEE

Block Party was an absolute joy to be a part of. These days, quilters rarely have best friends or neighbors who also quilt, and I am no exception. Where, then, does one go for inspiration and "quilt talk"? For me, it was straight to the Internet and the burgeoning online quilting community that resides there. One does not have to venture far within the Web to find an abundance of modern quilting talent and inspiration, and one of the most vibrant sources of modern quilting inspiration is virtual quilting bees. I was absolutely fortunate to find myself among the talented women who comprised the Block Party virtual quilting bee. What a pleasure it was to create and sew blocks for eleven quilters who share such a similar passion for quilting! It was a first for me, this virtual quilting bee, but it will not be my last, by any stretch of the imagination.

Megan Risse is a self-taught quilter who lives in a 100-year-old Philadelphia brownstone with her husband-to-be and two naughty cats. Her quilting aesthetic has been greatly influenced by the cache of handmade antique quilts left behind by her great-grandmother Willa Rudolph. When she is not quilting obsessively, she is knitting obsessively. She records her crafty exploits at www.philistinemade.com.

Photo by Michael McLaughlin

the hive mind:

BEE TIPS & SUGGESTIONS

General Bee Tips

From running Block Party and partaking in many other virtual quilting bees we have learned the ins and outs of bees! Here are some of our thoughts.

When asking bee members to make blocks for you, keep a balance between seeking uniformity of style and allowing room for creativity from the bee members. You do not want bee members to feel like they are just labor for your quilt, with no creative influence on it.

Want to be involved in a bee but concerned about the price of all that fabric? Send everyone a fat quarter of a solid fabric and have the members use their scraps as well. Quality solid fabrics can be found for less than $5 a yard, so it will cost you less than $20 to buy enough fabric for all twelve bee members.

Keep the mailers you get as you receive blocks. You will have to send everyone back lots of blocks, so why not reuse all the mailers? It is always better to recycle packaging!

Rather than sending fabric, you can set up a bee in which members just sew from their stashes. A way to do this and have the blocks all work together is to stick to a limited color palette. Why not all shades of your favorite color? Or maybe just two colors?

How to Keep a Happy Bee

A bee is a collaboration between twelve (or more!) people. As a result you are inevitably dealing with different personalities. Some people are very communicative, some less. Some people find it easy to keep up-to-date, some fall behind. What must be remembered throughout is that the bee is meant to be fun. That said, it is also a yearlong commitment, so take that into consideration when signing up for it. Make sure it is something you have time for.

BEING A GOOD BEE HOST

The most important tip we have on being a good bee host is to be a present host. Among your tasks are inviting the bee members to join and assembling and keeping the members' mailing addresses updated. You will also communicate any changes in the schedule and generally oversee things. If your bee will have a blog and/or a Flickr group, it is up to you to get it all set up. You should also send reminders to members when their month to mail out the fabric is around the corner.

BEING A GOOD BEE MEMBER

If you are a member, when sending your blocks include a little note or a little gift (everyone loves chocolate!) if you'd like. It always makes a virtual bee a little more personal. If you are receiving blocks, email members when you get their blocks in the mail, letting them know they arrived. If there is a bee blog or Flickr group, participate in it. Post photos of your blocks and comment on other people's work. The idea is to collaboratively make quilts, but it is more fun if everyone gets to know each other a bit as well.

If you are running behind on your blocks, simply drop an email to the person you are making them for. Everyone understands that life happens. Just communicate about where things stand. Nothing puts a damper on a bee more than having one member who doesn't return her blocks and therefore stops everyone from being able to assemble their quilts.

Do not stress about perfect blocks or making better blocks than other people. If you have fun making the blocks or learn a little something new about quilting, then the purpose has been served. Bees are supposed to be enjoyable—not a sewing stress.

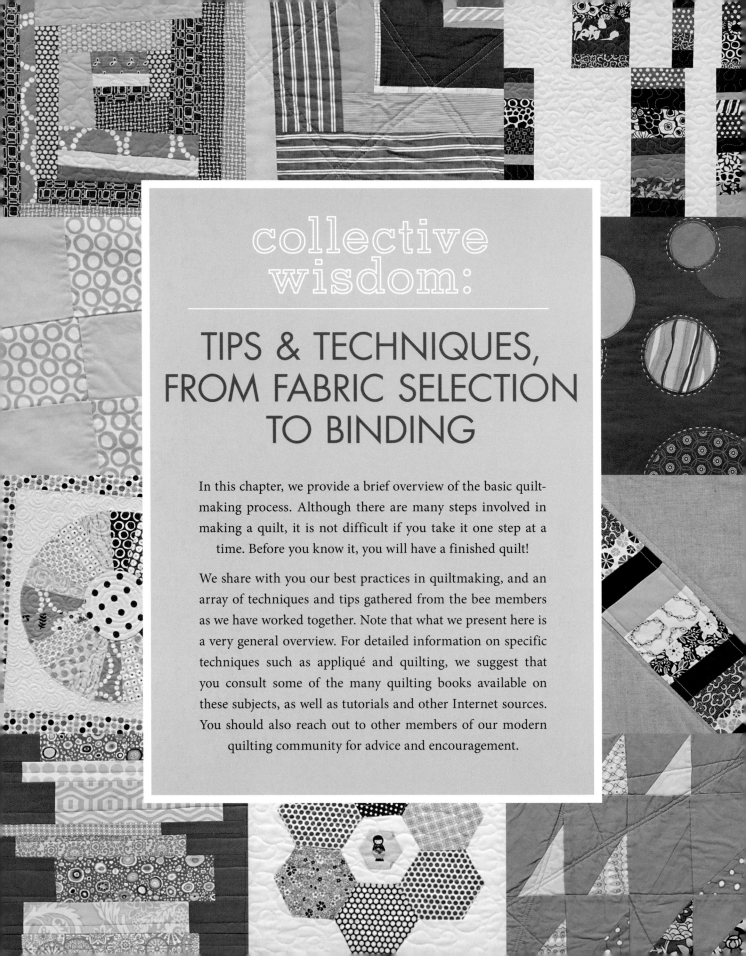

collective wisdom:

TIPS & TECHNIQUES, FROM FABRIC SELECTION TO BINDING

In this chapter, we provide a brief overview of the basic quilt-making process. Although there are many steps involved in making a quilt, it is not difficult if you take it one step at a time. Before you know it, you will have a finished quilt!

We share with you our best practices in quiltmaking, and an array of techniques and tips gathered from the bee members as we have worked together. Note that what we present here is a very general overview. For detailed information on specific techniques such as appliqué and quilting, we suggest that you consult some of the many quilting books available on these subjects, as well as tutorials and other Internet sources. You should also reach out to other members of our modern quilting community for advice and encouragement.

Modern Color Pairings

Color inspiration can come from anywhere—
a favorite piece of fabric, a vintage album cover, a flea market painting. Keep your eyes open for unexpected color pairings and jot them down. The vivid oranges and greens of the farmers' market or the cool pinks and grays of an antique piece of china may inspire the color choices for your next fabulous quilt.

Three basic color categories

Warm colors—reds, oranges, and yellows

Cool colors—blues and greens

Neutral colors—browns, tans, and grays

There are, of course, some colors that do not readily fit into these categories. (Fluorescents and metallics come to mind.) As a rule of thumb, anything that doesn't fit into one of these categories should be used sparingly, if at all!

Each quilt you make will demand a different mix of these three color categories. You can have a perfect balance of all three, use just two, or even go with only one. A quilt in all warms can be so beautiful (picture it in a bedroom with blue walls), but so can a scrappy quilt that's all the colors and shades of the rainbow. If you want to add more color range to a quilt, without taking away from its predominant color focus, adding a neutral works perfectly.

Modern Color Combinations

Raspberry and green grass   Orange and aqua   Goldenrod and gray

A good example of successful color pairings is Alissa's striking quilt *Once Around the Block*. Alissa chose patterned fabrics featuring one warm color (orange), one cool color (aqua), and one neutral color (gray). She added some aqua, gray, and white solids to balance the patterned fabrics.

Detail of *Once Around the Block* (page 17)

Selecting Fabrics

The fabrics you select for your quilt make all the difference. The smallest changes in your choices can have a huge impact on your quilt. Vibrancy, tone, and the overall impression your quilt makes are all decided by the fabrics you select.

FABRIC LINES

Quilting fabrics are typically released in collections, or lines, of fabrics. A line usually contains between four and eight different prints, in anywhere from two to four colorways (groups of coordinated colors). The prints are a mix of small-scale and large-scale motifs and may include some geometric designs, such as dots or stripes.

There is no denying the beauty of a wonderfully designed and coordinated fabric line—these fabrics are intended to go together. However, because the fabrics are all perfectly coordinated, a quilt made from only one fabric line can look a little flat. Also, using only one line leaves little room for you to use your creativity when picking out fabrics for your quilts.

We encourage you to mix and match from multiple fabric lines. Although it can take more time to make your choices, this will create a more interesting mix of prints, colors, and scales. A quilt can have more depth and range when you have put together an amazing fabric combination that won't be found in any other quilt.

When you are in fabric stores, take time to mix and match and pair fabrics that you do not instantly think work together. Then play with all the fabric in your stash. You never know what combinations you might discover you love.

SOLIDS AND PATTERNS

Another thing to consider when picking fabrics is the ratio of solid fabrics to patterned fabrics. Some people like all of one or the other. Or, try some of the other options shown here. Feature a bold pattern and mix it with solids to make the pattern pop. Or, use all solids to play up graphic shapes.

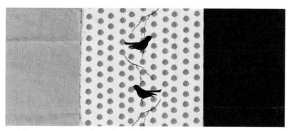

Bold pattern mixed with solids

All solids play up graphic shapes.

✳tip: To keep track of ideas for colors and designs, keep an "inspiration" notebook handy. When you are standing in front of your fabric stash or planning a new quilt, it is handy to have such a notebook from which to draw ideas. We also tend to snap photos of inspirations we stumble across in day-to-day life. You never know what will give you the next great quilt idea!

Inspirations

Inspiration fabric

✳tip: A great idea is to use a favorite piece of fabric as inspiration for choosing all the fabrics for your quilt. Why not pick a favorite that has lots of colors in it and try to find solids and fabrics from other lines that match all or some of those colors? You might surprise yourself with the fabrics you pick and just how much you like them. Sometimes it's not until you see them side by side that you realize they work well together.

Inspired mix 1

Also consider the size, or scale, of the pattern on the fabric. Will you be making a quilt that will have large pieces of fabric in it, or will you be piecing together many tiny pieces? A large-scale print will not work well if you will be cutting it up into small pieces, but a smaller-scale print would make that sort of piecing shine.

Inspired mix 2

Inspired mix 3

Small- and large-scale patterned fabrics

ALTERNATIVES TO QUILTING COTTONS

Most fabrics that are marketed for quilting are quilting cottons. However, there are many alternatives that will work well in a quilt.

You might try upholstery-weight fabrics, which tend to be heavier than quilting cottons. These will give your quilt a heavier feel and less drape. The fabrics are very durable and would work especially well for a picnic blanket.

Apparel fabrics—especially cotton fabrics such as twill, voile, eyelet, dobby, or seersucker—can also work well in quilting projects. Silk and satin can be difficult to sew with but can be beautiful accents on quilts. Linen is wonderful to quilt with, adding texture and drape.

Here are some helpful tips for working successfully with fabrics other than quilting cottons.

■ Within one quilt, stick to fabrics of similar weights. If you use lightweight voiles and heavy upholstery fabrics in the same quilt, the seams will not be very stable and may pull apart.

■ For fabrics that are slippery or shifty, such as linen or satin, it may help to use a lightweight fusible interfacing. The interfacing stabilizes the fabric and makes it much easier to sew.

■ Avoid knits, which tend to stretch and pull. If you use any knits, stabilize them with a lightweight interfacing prior to piecing.

■ Stick to natural fibers and avoid manmade fibers, such as polyester.

■ Pick fabrics appropriate to the quilt that you want to sew. For example, in a baby quilt, use fabrics that are washable and durable.

UPCYCLED FABRICS

Quilting has its roots in the idea of making a blanket out of materials that are available. Traditionally, quilts were made from outgrown or worn-out clothing and leftover fabric scraps—even feed sacks—so that nothing was wasted. Using up the extra bits and pieces of fabric that you have on hand is a wonderful way to be "green" and to end up with a beautiful result.

Some examples of commonly reused fabric are baby clothes, felted wool sweaters, old denim—or old, worn clothing of any kind. Nettie's wonderfully unique *Square Deal* quilt (page 24) is a great example of a quilt made from recycled men's shirts and ties.

T-shirts are another good source. Can't bear to get rid of your concert T-shirt collection? Turn it into a quilt! But be sure to do some research on the needs of the fabric you use. For example, a T-shirt quilt made from jersey knits will need to be stabilized.

Keep your eyes open at thrift stores, flea markets, and yard sales for amazing fabric finds. Clothing, sheets, and other linens can all provide interesting bits of fabric for a quilt.

Cutting Fabric

TOOLS

The primary tools to use when cutting fabric are a rotary cutter, a clear acrylic ruler, and a cutting mat. If you are new to quilting, these are some of the first tools you should buy. You can find them in affordable sets of all three or buy them separately at any good quilting or fabric store. You will use them all the time, and with a bit of practice they become very easy to use and invaluable.

Using a rotary cutter

Choose a rotary cutter that feels comfortable in your hand. Hold the cutter firmly in your dominant hand and use your other hand to hold the ruler in place. If your cutting table is the right height, you can put the weight of your body on the ruler to keep it in place. In one smooth, firm motion, starting at the bottom of the fabric, cut away from yourself.

Caution! The blade in the cutter is very sharp, so be careful. Always cut away from yourself to avoid pushing that sharp blade toward your body, and be sure to keep your fingers away from both the blade and your cutting line. Remember to close the blade when you are not using the rotary cutter, even if you are only pausing for a moment. *This rule is especially important if you have small children in the house.* Always, always close the blade.

Keep a sharp blade in your rotary cutter. When you find that one roll of the cutter isn't quite cutting through the fabric, it's time to replace the blade.

Rulers and cutting mat

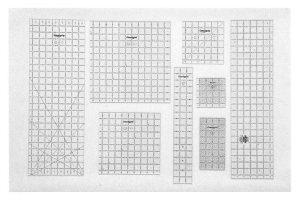

There are many different sizes of rulers available. We find most useful a 6″ × 24″ ruler, a 3″ × 18″ ruler, and a 12½″ square ruler.

Choose a "self-healing" cutting mat—preferably one that is 18″ × 24″ or larger. The mat should be big enough to allow you to work with various-sized pieces of fabric but small enough to fit on your work surface.

A cutting mat is printed with a grid that works as a ruler. You will use this grid to square up everything you sew, so become familiar with it. Because you will make hundreds and hundreds of cuts on this mat, it will not take long for you to wrap your head around the ins and outs of using the ruler and mat grid to make cuts.

Piecing

Piecing is the term for sewing together the bits and pieces of fabric that make up a quilt top. The more you piece, the better you will get at doing it.

Generally when piecing, you should use a seam that is at least ¼″ wide. This will ensure that your construction is solid and that the piecing will not come apart over time. Seams that are narrower than ¼″ may eventually pull and separate, especially on quilts that will be machine washed. However, you also do not want your seams to be too wide, as this will cause bulk and make it more difficult to quilt the top. Where seams are wider than ¾″, you should trim the extra width from the seams.

You will learn that there are times when you must be very careful and precise with your piecing, and times when you can be freer. To accurately piece many traditional patterns, you will need to learn to make an exact ¼″ seam. For other patterns, especially improvisational patterns, you need not worry about achieving perfect ¼″ seams. For example, with the wonky Log Cabin blocks, it makes no difference whether your seams are ¼″ or ⅜″.

SEWING ¼″ SEAMS

The standard seam allowance in quilting is a scant ¼″, which is just a few threads shy of a full ¼″. Many sewing machines come with a ¼″ piecing foot, which will help you with precise piecing. For some machines, it is an additional purchase, but it is well worth the cost.

Test your ¼″ seam by sewing together three 1½″ strips of fabric and pressing them. If your seams are actually a scant ¼″, the sewn strips will measure exactly 3½″ in width. If they do not measure 3½″, experiment with stitching a slightly wider or narrower seam until you achieve the right measurement. You can add a strip of tape on the throat plate of your machine to show where to line up the fabric for that perfect scant ¼″ seam.

SQUARING UP FABRIC

Squaring up your fabric ensures that any straight cuts you make will be along the grain of the fabric. *Grain* refers to the threads that run lengthwise and crosswise through the fabric. You want the grainlines to be at right angles with each other when you cut the fabric to prevent the fabric from twisting or pulling. You want your cuts to be straight.

To square up the fabric, fold it in half, taking care to carefully and evenly line up the selvages. Make sure that the fold of the fabric is even and not warped. Lay the folded fabric on your cutting mat with the selvages and fold lined up with horizontal lines on the mat. With a ruler and rotary cutter, trim one raw edge into a straight vertical line. Measure any subsequent cuts from this line.

Once you have squared up the fabric, you can cut with the fabric folded selvage to selvage. This is useful for making a very long cut or for cutting across the entire width of fabric. If you are cutting squares, you can cut strips that are the width the squares need to be and then stack strips before cutting them into squares.

Always use your ruler and cutting mat to square up blocks and quilt tops. Blocks can be centered over cutting-mat lines before being trimmed down. Be sure not to trim too much off one side—unless you want the block off-center for design reasons.

PINNING

When placed right sides together, fabrics tend to cling together somewhat. As a result, with many seams, particularly short ones, you may not need to pin—you can just sew away. With other seams, however, you will find that pinning is crucial. Long or curved seams will need to be pinned.

We like quilting pins that have flat heads, which allow the fabric to lie flat as you sew it together, but you may find another style of pin that will be your favorite.

When sewing along a pinned seam, you can often sew right over the pins and remove them after the entire seam has been sewn. Be cautious, however, when sewing over pins, as occasionally your needle may catch a pin, or the needle may even break. When this happens, take your foot off the pedal and manually raise the needle. Remove the offending pin, and, if necessary, change your sewing machine needle.

PRESSING

Pressing seams helps to set them and allows them to lie flat when you sew them to other pieced units. Pressing for quilting is different from ironing. Ironing—pushing the iron across the seams—can distort the fabric. Instead, you want to press and lift by placing the iron gently down, pressing the fabric to one side of the seam, and lifting the iron straight up.

When sewing quilt rows together, you should press the seams so the direction alternates from row to row. Use this same type of pressing when sewing a block together as well. Pressing seams in this manner will allow you to neatly match the seams when you sew two rows together. You can butt (or nest) the seams up against each other so they lie flat.

✳tip: Always press a seam before you sew across it. Pressing will make everything prettier and easier when you're quilting. There's an ongoing debate as to whether it is better to press seams to one side or to press seams open. This debate will likely never be resolved, and although people have strong feelings on the matter, it is up to you to decide which method you prefer. Both are good for different reasons. Pressing the seams open gives you a nice flat result, but pressing the seams to one side is quicker and easier. Try both, and with time you will decide which method works better for you.

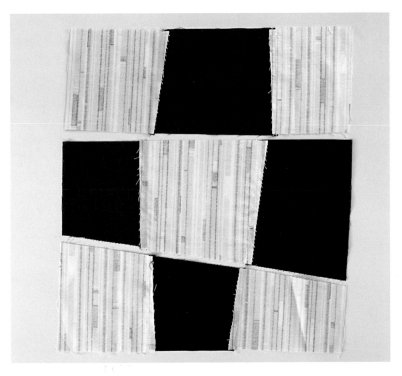

Appliqué

Appliqué is a sewing technique often used to create quilt blocks. In French, the word *appliqué* means "apply to," which describes the technique perfectly. Instead of piecing fabric together, you sew (apply) cut shapes onto a background fabric. Appliqué is particularly useful for adding circles (like those in Lisa's *Connect the Dots*, page 69) or small detailed shapes to your quilt blocks. You can explore a variety of appliqué methods that range from quick and easy, such as raw-edge and fused appliqué, to the fine art of exquisite needle-turn appliqué.

You can appliqué by machine or by hand. Machine sewing is much faster, but when you are machine sewing shapes to the background fabric there is simply no way to hide your stitches, as in the method shown in Rashida's *Specks of Hex* (page 83). We offer an alternative machine method for turning under seam allowances in Jacquie's *Profit Margins* (page 62), but in this method the stitching will also show. You can use invisible thread and/or a stitch that lends a decorative touch to machine appliqué. Some quilters prefer the invisible look that tiny hidden hand stitches provide.

You can find lots of information on specific appliqué methods on the Internet as well as in quilting books. Older sources might not have many patterns and looks that appeal to your modern quilting eye, but their practical advice is invaluable. You might find a whole new world opened to you when you combine your modern design sense with these very traditional skills.

Quilt Top Layouts

One of the most exciting parts of participating in a bee is figuring out how to combine into one quilt all the amazing blocks that you receive. The choice of block setting, or layout—the way in which you combine the blocks—can dramatically affect the look and size of your finished quilt.

To design the setting, place all the blocks in your proposed layout on a clean floor or large table. Review them to make sure all the blocks work well with each other. Be on the lookout for blocks that do not agree with one another—maybe they look too similar or they clash. Move the blocks around until you have found a layout that works. Sometimes snapping a photo of a layout and viewing it on the computer can help you see blocks that look out of place or don't quite fit in. Squinting your eyes while looking at the layout also gives you a better sense of the big picture and will make you notice if a block "pops" in an unattractive way. We just touch on a few layout ideas here that we used in our projects.

*tip: If you have a wall in your house that will accommodate it, a design wall can be invaluable for deciding on your block layout. You can make a simple design wall by tacking a flannel sheet or a big piece of 100% cotton batting to the wall. Fabric sticks to it like magic! You will find that your imagination and design ideas flow when you can leave something on the wall and come back to it later.

JUST BLOCKS   The simplest quilt layout features blocks of uniform size sewn directly to each other in rows. The blocks can be arranged into rows or columns.

Kristen's *Sliding By* (page 54) and Rashida's *Specks of Hex* (page 83) are good examples.

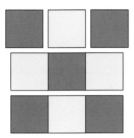

Just blocks layout

SASHING   A widely used method is to add sashing strips—usually of contrasting fabric—between blocks and rows. Take a look at Lisa's *Connect the Dots* (page 69) and Ashley's *Whole Nine Yards* (page 31) to see how contrasting sashing looks. You add short sashing strips between the blocks in each row, and you add long sashing strips between the rows. Make sure that your blocks are all the same size, determine the size for the short sashing strips, and cut each consistently. Then determine the correct length for the long sashing pieces and cut them all consistently. By adding sashing in the quilt layout, you can increase the finished size of your quilt. With sashing, you join the blocks and sashing

into rows. Then you join the rows, with the long sashing pieces between the rows.

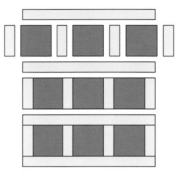

Sashing layout

FRAMING BLOCKS   To frame blocks, you essentially add borders to each individual block. Sewing strips of framing fabric around the edges of the blocks increases the size of the blocks. Framing works especially well when you are combining blocks that are not the same size or shape, like the blocks Alissa received for her quilt, *Once Around the Block* (page 17).

To frame irregularly sized blocks, first determine the final size that you want for the blocks. Then figure out the size of fabric strips you need to border the smallest block to achieve the desired dimensions. If you cut strips that size for all the blocks, you know the strips will be large enough. Border and trim your blocks to the same size.

You can wonky frame your blocks for a whimsical look, as Jacquie did in *Profit Margins* (page 62).

Even frame   Uneven frame   Wonky frame

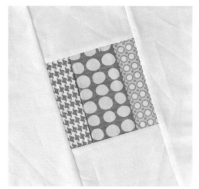

Steps for wonky frames

BORDERS   Once you decide on the layout for the blocks, you can add borders to the outside of your quilt, as Ashley did with *Falling to Pieces* (page 38). Borders create a frame around the entire quilt and can increase the size of the finished quilt.

ASSEMBLING YOUR QUILT TOP

You are ready to assemble the top now. At this point, it's helpful to label each block or sashing piece with a number, starting with 1 in the upper left-hand corner and continuing from left to right across each row. Then stack the blocks in numerical order, with 1 on top. This allows you to keep track of the quilt layout without worrying about the blocks getting moved around, being stepped on by a dog, or being absconded by a toddler!

Assemble the rows first. Move from the first block through to the last block at the end of the row, adding any sashing pieces between the blocks. As you complete each row, replace it in your design space and then assemble the next row. Once the rows are assembled, start sewing them to one another, working your way from top to bottom and adding the longer horizontal sashing pieces between the rows if necessary.

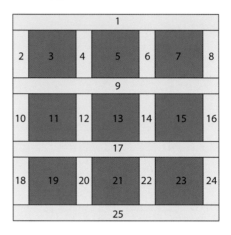

As you assemble the quilt top, be sure to use a consistent seam width and match up the seams as you move down the row. When sewing the long seams of one row to another, be extra generous with the pins. Pin at each seam intersection, making sure the seams match up, and pin between the seam intersections as well. If you pin like crazy, you will not have to worry about your blocks and sashing ending up misaligned.

Quilt Backs

The quilt back is just that—the piece of fabric that will be the back of your quilt. Eventually you will be creating a quilt sandwich, which is made up of an assembled quilt top, batting in the middle, and a quilt back.

Generally, the backing should be at least 8″ wider and longer than the quilt top. However, if you plan to send the quilt to a longarm quilter for quilting (see Longarm quilting, page 120), check with the quilter before making the backing.

ONE-FABRIC QUILT BACKS

Many quilters opt to use one pattern or color of fabric on the back because they prefer the uniform look.

With a small quilt, you may be able to use a single piece of standard-width quilting fabric, which is generally 42″ wide. With a larger quilt, however, you will not be able to use a single piece.

You can purchase specialty quilt-back fabric, which comes in widths of up to 110″, but unfortunately the color and pattern selections are limited. You can also piece together a quilt back from standard-width fabrics. We recommend choosing a nondirectional pattern or a solid, which will be easy to piece and will require less fabric than a directional print. Be sure to trim the selvages off all fabrics before joining them together. For quilts up to 80″ wide, you can use two widths of standard quilting fabric and seam them vertically. For quilts wider than 80″, you will need at least three widths of standard quilting fabric.

Another option is to use an appropriately sized 100% cotton flat bed sheet. Although quilters are traditionally warned against using sheets as backings, we have had great luck using higher-quality sheets with a high thread count as backings. Select a sheet with a similar feel to quilting fabric and one that you would like to snuggle up with. Prepare the sheet by washing it to eliminate any shrinkage and trimming off the hemmed edges.

FREESTYLE PIECED QUILT BACKS

Rather than the traditional one-fabric back, many quilters prefer to use multiple fabrics in their quilt backs—these look interesting and allow you to use up large scraps of leftover fabric from the top.

To create a freestyle back, first determine the final size of the quilt back. Next find one or two larger pieces of fabric that you can piece together that will make up a large portion of the back. Piece together narrow or wide strips of coordinating fabrics and add them to these larger pieces. Consider adding extra blocks or scraps left over from the quilt top.

*tip: Press every time you add another piece! It is very important that all the seams be pressed flat; otherwise you may end up with bumps and ripples on the back of the quilt.

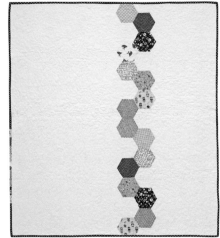

Nettie's *Square Deal* (page 24) and Rashida's *Specks of Hex* (page 83) feature some blocks from their quilt tops.

FREESTYLE PIECED BACKS

Ashley's *Falling to Pieces* (page 38) and Kristen's *Sliding By* (page 54) make use of leftover bits from the quilt tops to create larger quilt backs. Kristen added a whimsical bird print.

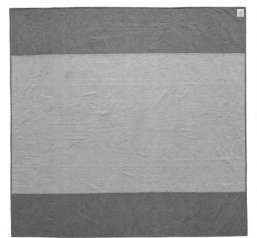

Lisa's *Connect the Dots* (page 69) and Elizabeth's *Earn Your Stripes* (page 89) have backs pieced together from widths of coordinating fabrics.

The Quilt Sandwich

The quilt "sandwich" is made up of the quilt top and back with a layer of soft filler, or batting, in between. You will need to secure together all three layers so they don't shift while you quilt them.

BATTING

Batting adds weight and warmth to your finished quilt. The type of batting you use can dramatically affect the quilt's look and feel. No matter what type you use, the batting should be approximately 6″ longer and wider than the quilt top.

Batting comes in many different thicknesses and textures and can be composed of many different types of fibers. With any batting, follow the manufacturer's recommendations regarding washing and quilting. Here's a short list of types of batting now available:

- Cotton batting
- Wool batting
- Cotton/wool blend batting
- "Green" batting such as bamboo/cellulose and batting made from recycled materials
- Silk batting
- Polyester batting

For a thinner batting layer, you can also use cotton flannel, polyester fleece, or even old woolen blankets.

Natural fibers such as cotton and wool are soft and have a wonderful drape. Polyester battings are lightweight and can lend a fluffy look to a quilt. We tend to prefer natural fibers for the drape and breathability.

tip: If not preshrunk, some battings such as cotton will give your quilt a crinkly look after it is machine washed. We love this look, so we never preshrink our battings, but you can preshrink if you prefer a less-crinkled finished product. Before preshrinking your batting, read the manufacturer's recommendations.

ASSEMBLING THE LAYERS

You'll find yourself crawling around on the floor for these steps, so sweep, close those pets away, and get started!

1. Lay out the quilt back wrong side up on a flat surface such as a clean floor. Secure the edges to the floor with masking tape. Pull the edges taut, but do not stretch or distort the fabric.

2. Center the batting in the middle of the backing, and smooth out all the wrinkles. You may find it helpful to roll the batting into a tube and, starting at one end of the backing, unroll the batting and smooth out the wrinkles, lumps, and bumps as you go.

3. With the right side up, center the pressed quilt top over the batting, smoothing out the wrinkles.

BASTING

You will need to baste the quilt sandwich together unless you are taking the quilt top to a longarm machine quilter or tying the quilt top. For hand quilting or machine quilting on your home machine, thorough basting will ensure that you have no wrinkles on the quilt top or back after quilting. If you are pin basting or thread basting, work from the center outward, smoothing wrinkles and pinning or stitching as you go.

Try out these three popular methods to figure out what works best for you and your quilts:

- Hand basting with a needle and thread using very large stitches, working from the center out and smoothing wrinkles as you stitch

- Safety pins placed every 4″ to 6″ apart, working from the center out and smoothing wrinkles as you go

- Basting spray, following the manufacturer's instructions

Hand basting with large stitches   Safety pins every 4″ to 6″

*tip: When you remove the safety pins from the quilt, leave them open. No need to double your work by closing them when you will just need to open them up again when you baste your next quilt!

Quilting

Quilting is the process of sewing together the layers of the quilt sandwich. It also adds wonderful dimension and texture to an already beautiful quilt top. Here we first provide information on tying your quilt—a quick and easy method of quilting. We present a quick overview of machine and hand quilting as well. To learn more about quilting, refer to Internet tutorials and the wealth of excellent books available on the subject.

We generally do not mark our quilts for quilting. We often stipple our quilts if we are machine quilting, which is a freehand design, or we use straight-line quilting, which does not require marking. If we are tying our quilts, we like to use the piecing or the fabric pattern to determine where we will make the ties. If you decide on a quilt design that requires marking, check with your local quilt shop for marking methods and the tools that are needed. The Internet is also a good resource for methods and marking tools such as pencils, chalk, and water-soluble markers, as well as stencils and rulers.

TYING

Tying is the easiest, quickest way to join the layers of a quilt sandwich, and the basting step is not required. It is simple, functional, and attractive. You need only a tapestry needle and yarn or perle cotton in a color that complements your quilt top. Refer to the batting manufacturer's instructions to see how close the quilting needs to be so that you can plan the ties close enough together for the type of batting you are using.

1. Lay the quilt sandwich flat. Thread a long piece of yarn in the needle, but do not tie a knot in the end. Starting in the center of the quilt, insert the needle from the top of the quilt through the entire quilt sandwich and back up. Leaving the ties uncut, work your way down the center of the quilt. Evenly space the ties, coordinating the placement with your quilt design. Leave no more than 4″ to 8″ between ties.

2. After you have covered the entire quilt, snip the ties. Finish each with a sturdy square knot or surgeon's knot, pulling firmly. Trim the ties to about 1″ long.

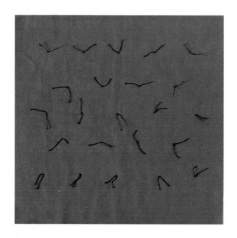

Ashley tied her wonky Nine-Patch quilt, giving it a simple soft appeal.

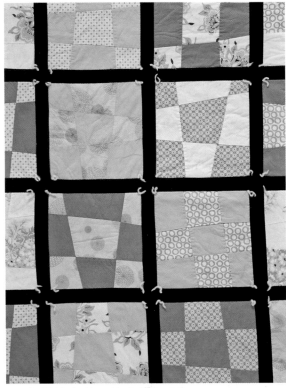

Detail of *Whole Nine Yards* (page 31)

QUILTING DESIGNS

Straight lines, allover squiggles, and planned patterns are all possibilities for quilting designs, whether you are machine quilting or hand quilting. Study your quilt top to determine what quilting pattern would complement it. Straight-line quilting designs are geometric and clean looking. Meandering and other overall designs will allow the design of the quilt top to stand out, rather than the quilting. Motifs that echo the design of the top can create an emphasis on certain aspects of your quilt design and showcase favorite blocks or motifs.

HAND QUILTING

Hand quilting is an art form, and mastering the techniques of hand quilting can take a lifetime. Here, rather than focusing on tiny perfect stitches made with quilting thread, we used a larger stitch and thicker thread such as perle cotton to emphasize the organic stitches of a beginning hand quilter. For larger quilts, where hand quilting might seem impractical (or impossible!), consider using hand stitching as an accent to highlight certain details in your quilt. If you want to learn more about hand quilting, refer to one of the many books available on this subject.

Lisa hand quilted her polka dot quilt (page 69) using large stitches in contrasting thread to outline the dots.

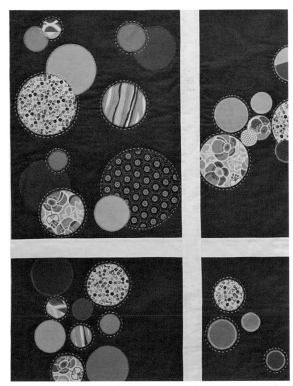

Detail of Lisa's quilt (page 69)

The basic tools you'll need are simple—just a short, sharp quilter's needle; cotton quilting thread, perle cotton, or embroidery floss; a thimble; and a quilting hoop or frame. These steps show hand quilting on a small block.

1. Decide on a quilting design and, if necessary, mark your design on the quilt with chalk or a nonpermanent fabric marker. We chose a straight-line design for this block.

✳tip: Always, always, test your marking method to ensure that it will easily wash out of the fabric used in your quilt. Better safe than sorry!

----

2. We used safety pins to baste the layers of the block together. Place the center of the quilt in a hoop or frame, centering (as best you can) the portion you wish to quilt. You don't want the basting pins within the hoop. Thread your needle with about 18″ to 24″ of thread and knot one end. If using perle cotton or embroidery floss, pull 2 to 3 threads from the strand. To bury the

knot, insert the needle down through the top and batting and come back to the surface. Give the thread a firm tug to pull the knot between the layers.

3. Put the thimble on the middle or index finger of your dominant hand. Place the index finger of your other hand underneath the quilt. Use the thimble to rock the needle back and forth, catching all 3 layers of the quilt sandwich with small running stitches.

4. When your thread gets too short, tie another knot and bury it in the quilt sandwich as before. Continue quilting the area within the hoop and then reposition the hoop to the next area. Continue to reposition the hoop to complete the quilting.

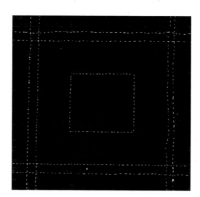

MACHINE QUILTING

Machine quilting can be done on a longarm machine or on almost any home sewing machine. For either, you can choose straight-line quilting or free-motion quilting designs to complement your quilt top. If you choose to use your home sewing machine and you are a beginner, straight-line quilting provides the most straightforward introduction to machine quilting. Although machine quilting is not difficult to learn, we suggest you consult books and Internet sources for details about machine quilting; they offer many tips and techniques—from the right way to begin your stitches to how to handle your quilt as you sew—that will help you succeed.

Straight-line quilting

The most important tool for this style of machine quilting is a walking foot, which prevents the fabric from bunching as you sew. The geometric designs you can achieve with this type of quilting complement many modern quilt designs.

You may use a fabric marker to mark quilting lines on your quilt, or you may do as many quilters do and use masking tape to mark the straight lines.

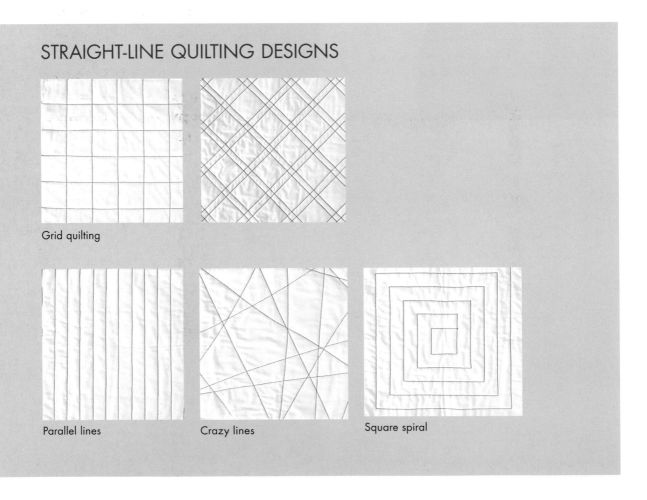

STRAIGHT-LINE QUILTING DESIGNS

Grid quilting

Parallel lines

Crazy lines

Square spiral

Free-motion quilting

Free-motion quilting will give your quilts a professionally quilted look and allow you to create an unlimited variety of designs. It is much easier than it seems; you will only need practice to become comfortable with it.

To free-motion quilt on your home machine, a darning or a free-motion foot is essential. This attachment will almost always have a circular foot and a spring that moves the foot up and down as you sew. When you quilt, you will need to lower your machine's feed dogs. If they don't lower, you may be able to cover them with an index card taped to the bed of the machine.

Most beginners start with stippling, a continuous curvy design that meanders across the quilt. Because it is intended to look random, stippling gives you a lot of room for error. Alissa stippled her very large quilt on her home machine.

To free-motion quilt, you use the needle to "draw" on the fabric, just like with pen and paper, but here the paper (quilt) moves and the pen (needle) stays stationary. Your stitch length is determined by the speed at which you move your hands. If you move the fabric quickly you will create large stitches; moving slowly will create small stitches. The key to free-motion quilting is to find the right balance between the speed the needle moves and the speed you move your quilt.

You will need to check the front and back of your stitching to see if the machine tension needs adjusting. Most quilters increase their tension while machine quilting. The tension should look the same front and back with no pulling of the bobbin thread to the front or loops on the back. If you are seeing uneven tension, you will need to adjust your tension. For help with the tension, consult your machine's manual. Check the tension early and often as you quilt to avoid having to pull out your machine quilting.

Detail of *Once Around the Block* (page 17)

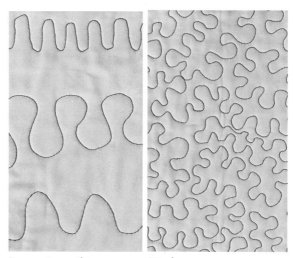

Free-motion quilting   Stippling

OUR FAVORITE FREE-MOTION TIPS

- If you have the feature on your machine, set your needle to stop in the down position so that you can stop and start as much as you need to without skipping around. If your machine doesn't have this feature, just remember to always roll the needle into the down position when you want to pause to rearrange your quilt.

- Plan your way of working through the quilt in advance. You always want to have as little of the quilt in the throat of your machine as possible. It is not always easy to squeeze a big quilt through a little machine, but it can be done!

- Pull the bobbin thread to the front of the quilt before you start stitching. This keeps you from sewing it into your quilting or creating a tangled mess of thread on the back of the quilt. You need to start and stop with some securing stitches. If you run out of thread in the bobbin while you are in the middle of your quilt, refill the bobbin and keep going from the same spot, making sure to sew a few locking stitches over where you left off.

- When you are quilting a large quilt, it helps to have table space both behind and to the left of your sewing machine to hold some of the weight of the quilt. An extension table, if available for your machine, is also very helpful in maneuvering a large quilt.

- The single biggest tip we can share for free-motion quilting on your home sewing machine is to practice on a "sandwich" scrap. Practice, practice, practice! The more you do it the more you will learn the ins and outs of your machine, and the smoother and better your quilting will become. Do not be scared. Start on something small and dive in! With some practice, you will be a pro in no time.

Longarm quilting

A longarm quilting machine is a large, expensive sewing machine on a frame that allows the quilter to move the sewing machine, essentially drawing the quilting on the fabric. Many quilters who own longarm machines offer quilting services. You package up your quilt top, batting, and quilt back, and deliver them to the longarm quilter. You get back a beautifully quilted quilt, with only the binding left to complete. For those of us who have limited time or who enjoy piecing more than quilting, longarm services are wonderful.

*tip: One of the major benefits of sending your quilt to a longarm machine quilter is that you do not have to assemble the quilt sandwich. With a longarm system, the quilt top, batting, and quilt back are all loaded independently onto rollers, so no basting is needed.

When choosing a longarm quilting service, ask these important questions:

- What is the turnaround time? Will the quilter guarantee that your quilt will be returned by a certain date?

- Does the quilter use computerized patterns? Or does this quilter do more heirloom quilting that is customized to your quilt pattern?

- How is the service priced? Usually the price is based on the square inches to be quilted and the complexity of the quilting pattern. Typically, custom heirloom quilting will cost more than an overall computer-generated pattern.

- Can the quilter provide references? Be especially careful when choosing a quilting service through the Internet.

Kristen and Jacquie sent their quilts out to longarm quilters. Kristen chose an overall meandering leaf pattern; Jacquie requested custom quilting that echoed the Dresden Plates in her quilt.

Kristen's *Sliding By* (page 54)

Jacquie's *Profit Margins* (page 62)

Binding

Like a beautiful picture frame, a well-done binding will showcase your quilt top.

The technique we demonstrate here is called double-fold French binding.

Binding strips can be cut on the straight of the fabric grain or on the bias (across the diagonal of the grain). Straight-grain binding uses less fabric than bias binding and works well on straight quilt edges. With a striped fabric, bias binding can look more interesting. If your quilt has any curved edges you must use bias binding, which will stretch to wrap nicely along a curve.

CHOOSING BINDING FABRIC

Choose a fabric that complements the overall look and feel of the finished quilt top.

You can pull one of the colors or patterns from your quilt top. FIGURE 1: Kristen used a solid chartreuse green fabric from her wonky Roman Stripe blocks. FIGURE 2: Josie picked one of the small-scale patterns from her String-X blocks.

You may choose to add a new color into the mix, creating contrast between the quilt top and the binding. FIGURE 3: Although Nettie's quilt featured fabrics in shades of blue and gold, she picked a fresh green dot for the binding.

You can also include more than one fabric in your binding. FIGURE 4: Megan used multiple patterns in the same color family. FIGURE 5: Elizabeth added a few small pieces of patterned fabric to her solid brown binding.

If you use a patterned fabric, keep in mind that it will be folded into a narrow binding, so a small-scale print will read better than a larger-scale print.

FIGURE 6: Rashida used a small white-on-red polka dot, which works nicely with her red, yellow, and blue quilt.

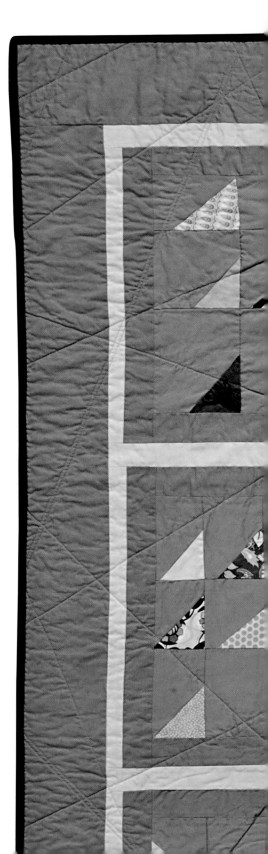

binding choices

[Figure 1]

[Figure 2]

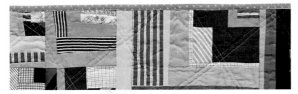

[Figure 3]

[Figure 4]

[Figure 5]

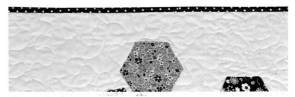

[Figure 6]

PREPARING STRAIGHT-GRAIN BINDING

We cut our binding strips 2½″ wide, so they finish to a ½″ binding.

1. Cut enough 2½″ strips (selvage to selvage) to go around the perimeter of your quilt plus an extra 12″ or so for corners.

2. Join the strips using a ½″ diagonal seam. Trim and press.

Preparing bias binding

This method of cutting continuous bias binding strips can change your quilting life. It takes some faith to get past the twisty tube, but it is worth it, we promise!

Essentially, you will slice a right triangle from a rectangle of binding fabric and sew the two pieces into a parallelogram so you can cut continuous strips.

1. Start with a rectangle of fabric. Draw a 45° line from one corner to the edge of the fabric and then cut on the line as shown. You have cut a right triangle.

2. Move the triangle to the other side of the fabric, keeping it oriented in the same direction. Sew the 2 pieces together as shown, using a ¼″ seam, to create the parallelogram. Press the seam open.

3. Starting at the left 45° edge, draw lines parallel to the cut edge, spaced 2½″ apart on the back of the fabric. Mark the lines with a pencil or an air-soluble marker and number them as shown.

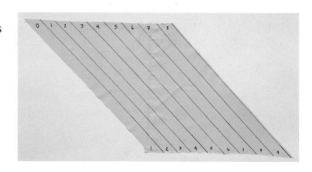

4. Now connect the 2 long edges, offsetting the join by the width of 1 strip. Pin along the 2 edges, matching up the lines and numbers as you go. Sew a ¼″ seam where you have just pinned and then press the seam open. You will have a twisted tube of fabric.

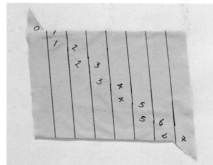

5. Starting at one end, cut along the drawn line. This is now a single long continuous line. You will cut in a spiral and end up with a bias strip!

✳**tip:** A yard of fabric will make about 550″ of 2½″ binding; ½ yard will make about 300″.

ATTACHING THE BINDING

1. Fold the binding in half lengthwise, right sides together, and press along the entire length.

2. Prepare your quilt by trimming off excess batting and backing even with the edges of the quilt top. You may find that basting along the entire quilt edge with a zigzag stitch, no more than ⅛″ from the edge, will help secure all 3 layers of the quilt sandwich.

3. Working from the front of the quilt, start in the middle of one side and leave a 10″ tail of binding. Align the raw edges of the binding with the raw edge of the quilt. Some quilters pin the binding in place first. We always stitch a ⅜″ seam, using the walking foot, to sew the binding to the quilt. However, if you have a traditional block (a Pinwheel block, for example), you will need to use a ¼″ seam so that you do not lose the points in the blocks.

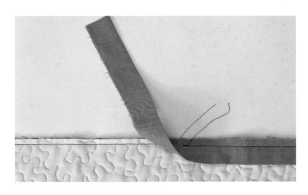

4. Stop stitching ⅜″ (if you are using a ⅜″ seam, but ¼″ if you are using a ¼″ seam) from the corner. To make a mitered corner, backstitch a stitch and lift the presser foot and needle. Remove the quilt from the machine and rotate the quilt a quarter turn. Fold the binding at a right angle so it extends straight above the quilt and the fold forms a 45° angle in the corner. Then bring the binding strip down, aligning the edge of the binding with the edge of the quilt. Begin sewing at the folded edge. Repeat in the same manner at all corners.

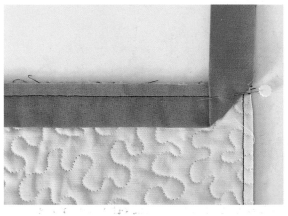

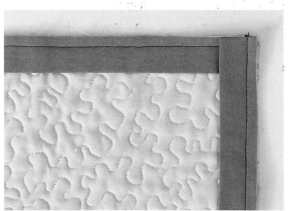

5. Once you have turned the last corner, stitch to within 20″ of your original starting point. Lay the 2 tails smoothly along the edge and trim so that they overlap by 2½″.

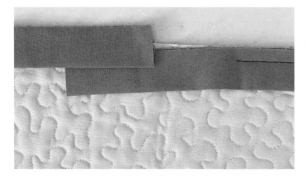

6. Now place the 2 ends right sides together and perpendicular to each other. Overlap the ends slightly and pin. Draw a diagonal line as shown and stitch along this line.

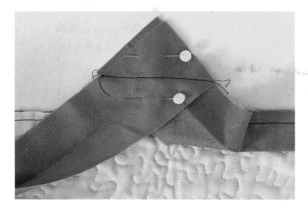

7. Trim the excess fabric, press the seam, and refold the binding in half. Realign the raw edges of the binding with the edge of the quilt and stitch the remaining binding to the quilt.

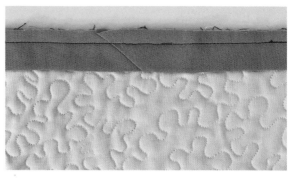

✳**tip:** Before you fold the binding toward the back, you can press the binding toward the raw edge of the quilt to keep the fold nice and even.

- -

8. Fold the binding to the back of the quilt, over the raw edges of the quilt, and pin or clip it in place if you wish. Hand stitch the folded edge to the quilt back using a blind stitch and hiding the machine stitching line. When you reach a corner, fold the binding in a neat miter and secure it with a few stitches.

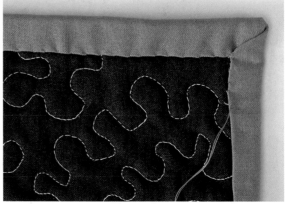

ABOUT THE AUTHORS

ALISSA HAIGHT CARLTON lives in Los Angeles with her filmmaker husband. She has been obsessively quilting for four years. She is one of the founders of the Modern Quilt Guild. When not quilting, she casts reality TV shows, including seasons seven and eight of *Project Runway*. She blogs about her quilting at www.handmadebyalissa.com.

KRISTEN LEJNIEKS is an attorney currently living in Washington, D.C., with her husband and two daughters (ages two and three). She loves to bite off more than she can chew, whether it be starting a quilt three days before a baby shower or agreeing to write a book while working full-time. Kristen blogs (sporadically) at www.kristenunraveled.com.

For a list of other fine books from C&T Publishing, visit our website to view our catalog online.

C&T PUBLISHING, INC.
P.O. Box 1456
Lafayette, CA 94549
800-284-1114

Email: ctinfo@ctpub.com
Website: www.ctpub.com

C&T Publishing's professional photography services are now available to the public. Visit us at www.ctmediaservices.com.

Tips and Techniques can be found at www.ctpub.com > Consumer Resources > Quiltmaking Basics: Tips & Techniques for Quiltmaking & More

For quilting supplies:

COTTON PATCH
1025 Brown Ave.
Lafayette, CA 94549
Store: 925-284-1177
Mail order: 925-283-7883

Email: CottonPa@aol.com
Website: www.quiltusa.com

Note: Fabrics used in the quilts shown may not be currently available, as fabric manufacturers keep most fabrics in print for only a short time.

s1

fabric

If y
of
Boo
for
soli
you
inst